Do Connecticut

The 57 Best Places To Hike With Your Dog In The Nutmeg State

DOUG GELBERT

illustrations by

ANDREW CHESWORTH

Cruden Bay Books

There is always a new trail to look forward to...

DOGGIN' CONNECTICUT: THE 57 BEST PLACES TO HIKE
WITH YOUR DOG IN THE NUTMEG STATE

Cruden Bay Books
PO Box 467
Montchanin, DE 19710
www.hikewithyourdog.com

International Standard Book Number 978-0-9797074-6-9

*"Dogs are our link to paradise...to sit with a dog on a hillside
on a glorious afternoon is to be back in Eden,
where doing nothing was not boring - it was peace."*
- Milan Kundera

Ahead On The Trail

Introduction

Connecticut can be a great place to hike with your dog. Within a short drive your canine adventurer can be climbing hills that leave him panting, trotting on some of the most historic grounds in America, exploring the estates of America's wealthiest families or circling lakes for miles and never lose sight of the water.

I have selected what I consider to be the 57 best places to take your dog for an outing in Connecticut and ranked them according to subjective criteria including the variety of hikes available, opportunities for canine swimming and pleasure of the walks. The rankings include a mix of parks that feature long walks and parks that contain short walks. Did I miss your favorite? Let us know at *www.hikewithyourdog. com.*

For dog owners it is important to realize that not all parks are open to our best trail companions (see page 14 for a list of parks that do not allow dogs). It is sometimes hard to believe but not everyone loves dogs. We are, in fact, in the minority when compared with our non-dog owning neighbors.

So when visiting a park always keep your dog under control and clean up any messes and we can all expect our great parks to remain open to our dogs. And maybe some others will see the light as well. *Remember, every time you go out with your dog you are an ambassador for all dog owners.*

Grab that leash and hit the trail!
DBG

Hiking With Your Dog

So you want to start hiking with your dog. Hiking with your dog can be a fascinating way to explore the Nutmeg State from a canine perspective. Some things to consider:

🐾 Dog's Health

Hiking can be a wonderful preventative for any number of physical and behavioral disorders. One in every three dogs is overweight and running up trails and leaping through streams is great exercise to help keep pounds off. Hiking can also relieve boredom in a dog's routine and calm dogs prone to destructive habits. And hiking with your dog strengthens the overall owner/dog bond.

🐾 Breed of Dog

All dogs enjoy the new scents and sights of a trail. But some dogs are better suited to hiking than others. If you don't as yet have a hiking companion, select a breed that matches your interests. Do you look forward to an entire afternoon's hiking? You'll need a dog bred to keep up with such a pace, such as a retriever or a spaniel. Is a half-hour enough walking for you? It may not be for an energetic dog like a border collie. If you already have a hiking friend, tailor your plans to his abilities.

🐾 Conditioning

Just like humans, dogs need to be acclimated to the task at hand. An inactive dog cannot be expected to bounce from the easy chair in the den to complete a 3-hour hike. You must also be physically able to restrain your dog if confronted with distractions on the trail (like a scampering squirrel or a pack of joggers). Have your dog checked by a veterinarian before significantly increasing his activity level.

🐾 Weather

Hot humid summers do not do dogs any favors. With no sweat glands and only panting available to disperse body heat, dogs are much more susceptible to heat stroke than we are. Unusually rapid panting and/or a bright red tongue are signs of heat exhaustion in your pet.

Always carry enough water for your hike. Even days that don't seem too warm can cause discomfort in dark-coated dogs if the sun is shining brightly. In cold weather, short-coated breeds may require additional attention.

🐾 Trail Hazards

Dogs won't get poison ivy but they can transfer it to you. Some trails are littered with small pieces of broken glass that can slice a dog's paws. Nasty thorns can also blanket trails that we in shoes may never notice. At the beach beware of sand spurs that can often be present in scrubby, sandy areas.

🐾 Ticks

You won't be able to spend much time in Connecticut woods without encountering ticks. All are nasty but the deer tick - no bigger than a pin head - carries with it the spectre of Lyme disease. Lyme disease attacks a dog's joints and makes walking painful. The tick needs to be embedded in the skin to transmit Lyme disease. It takes 4-6 hours for a tick to become embedded and another 24-48 hours to transmit Lyme disease bacteria.

When hiking, walk in the middle of trails away from tall grass and bushes. And when the summer sun fades away don't stop thinking about ticks - they remain active any time the temperature is above 30 degrees. By checking your dog - and yourself - thoroughly after each walk you can help avoid Lyme disease. Ticks tend to congregate on your dog's ears, between the toes and around the neck and head.

🐾 Water

Surface water, including fast-flowing streams, is likely to be infested with a microscopic protozoa called *Giardia*, waiting to wreak havoc on a dog's intestinal system. The most common symptom is crippling diarrhea. Algae, pollutants and contaminants can all be in streams, ponds and puddles. If possible, carry fresh water for your dog on the trail - your dog can even learn to drink happily from a squirt bottle.

At the beach, cool sea water will be tempting for your dog but try to limit any drinking as much as possible. Again, have plenty of fresh water available for your dog to drink instead.

Rattlesnakes and Copperheads, etc.

Rattlesnakes and their close cousins, copperheads, are not particularly aggressive animals but you should treat any venomous snake with respect and keep your distance. A rattler's colors may vary but they are recognized by the namesake rattle on the tail and a diamond-shaped head. Unless cornered or teased by humans or dogs, a rattlesnake will crawl away and avoid striking. Avoid placing your hand in unexamined rocky areas and crevasses and try and keep your dog from doing so as well. Stick to the trail and out of high grass where you can't see well. If you hear a nearby rattle, stop immediately and hold your dog back. Identify where the snake is and slowly back away.

If you or your dog is bitten, do not panic but get to a hospital or veterinarian with as little physical movement as possible. Wrap between the bite and the heart. Rattlesnakes might give "dry bites" where no poison is injected, but you should always check with a doctor after a bite even if you feel fine.

Black Bears

Are you likely to see a bear while out hiking with your dog? No, it's not likely. It is, however, quite a thrill if you are fortunate enough to spot a black bear on the trail - from a distance.

Black bear attacks are incredibly rare. In the year 2000 a hiker was killed by a black bear in Great Smoky National Park and it was the first deadly bear attack in the 66-year history of America's most popular national park. It was the first EVER in the southeastern United States. In all of North America only 43 black bear mauling deaths have ever been recorded (through 1999).

Most problems with black bears occur near a campground (like the above incident) where bears have learned to forage for unprotected food. On the trail bears will typically see you and leave the area. What should you do if you encounter a black bear? Experts agree on three important things:

1) Never run. A bear will outrun you, outclimb you, outswim you. Don't look like prey.
2) Never get between a female bear and a cub who may be nearby feeding.
3) Leave a bear an escape route.

If the bear is at least 15 feet away and notices you make sure you keep your dog close and calm. If a bear stands on its hind legs or comes closer it may just be trying to get a better view or smell to evaluate the situation. Wave your arms and make noise to scare the bear away. Most bears will quickly leave the area.

If you encounter a black bear at close range, stand upright and make yourself appear as large a foe as possible. Avoid direct eye contact and speak in a calm, assertive and assuring voice as you back up slowly and out of danger.

Porcupines

Porcupines are easy for a curious dog to catch and that makes them among the most dangerous animals you may meet because an embedded quill is not only painful but can cause infection if not properly removed.

Outfitting Your Dog For A Hike

These are the basics for taking your dog on a hike:

▸ **Collar.**
It should not be so loose as to come off but you should be able to slide your flat hand under the collar.

▸ **Identification Tags.**
Get one with your veterinarian's phone number as well.

▸ **Bandanna.**
Can help distinguish him from game in hunting season.

▸ **Leash.**
Leather lasts forever but if there's water in your dog"s future, consider quick-drying nylon.

▸ **Water.**
Carry 8 ounces for every hour of hiking.

🐾 *I want my dog to help carry water, snacks and other supplies on the trail. Where do I start?*

To select an appropriate dog pack measure your dog's girth around the rib cage. A dog pack should fit securely without hindering the dog's ability to walk normally.

🐾 *Will my dog wear a pack?*

Wearing a dog pack is no more obtrusive than wearing a collar, although some dogs will take to a pack easier than others. Introduce the pack by draping a towel over your dog's back in the house and then having your dog wear an empty pack on short walks. Progressively add some crumpled newspaper and then bits of clothing. Fill the pack with treats and reward your dog from the stash. Soon your dog will associate the dog pack with an outdoor adventure and will eagerly look forward to wearing it.

How much weight can I put into a dog pack?

Many dog packs are sold by weight recommendations. A healthy, well-conditioned dog can comfortably carry 25% to 33% of its body weight. Breeds prone to back problems or hip dysplasia should not wear dog packs. Consult your veterinarian before stuffing the pouches with gear.

How does a dog wear a pack?

The pack, typically with cargo pouches on either side, should ride as close to the shoulders as possible without limiting movement. The straps that hold the dog pack in place should be situated where they will not cause chafing.

What are good things to put in a dog pack?

Low density items such as food and poop bags are good choices. Ice cold bottles of water can cool your dog down on hot days. Don't put anything in a dog pack that can break. Dogs will bang the pack on rocks and trees as they wiggle through tight spots in the trail. Dogs also like to lie down in creeks and other wet spots so seal items in plastic bags. A good use for dog packs when on day hikes around Connecticut is trail maintenance - your dog can pack out trash left by inconsiderate visitors before you.

❖ *Are dog booties a good idea?*

Dog booties can be an asset, especially for the occasional canine hiker whose paw pads have not become toughened. In some places, there may be broken glass. Hiking boots for dogs are designed to prevent pads from cracking while trotting across rough surfaces. Used in winter, dog booties provide warmth and keep ice balls from forming between toe pads when hiking through snow.

❖ *What should a doggie first aid kit include?*

Even when taking short hikes it is a good idea to have some basics available for emergencies:

▸ 4" square gauze pads
▸ cling type bandaging tapes
▸ topical wound disinfectant cream
▸ tweezers
▸ insect repellent - no reason to leave your dog unprotected against mosquitoes and yellow flies
▸ veterinarian's phone number

"I can't think of anything that brings me closer to tears than
when my old dog - completely exhausted after a hard day
in the field - limps away from her nice spot in front of the fire
and comes over to where I'm sitting and puts her head in my lap,
a paw over my knee, and closes her eyes, and goes back to sleep.
I don't know what I've done to deserve that kind of friend."
-Gene Hill

Low Impact Hiking With Your Dog

Every time you hike with your dog on the trail you are an ambassador for all dog owners. Some people you meet won't believe in your right to take a dog on the trail. Be friendly to all and make the best impression you can by practicing low impact hiking with your dog:

- Pack out everything you pack in.

- Do not leave dog scat on the trail; if you haven't brought plastic bags for poop removal bury it away from the trail and topical water sources.

- Hike only where dogs are allowed.

- Stay on the trail.

- Do not allow your dog to chase wildlife.

- Step off the trail and wait with your dog while horses and other hikers pass.

- Do not allow your dog to bark - people are enjoying the trail for serenity.

- *Have as much fun on your hike as your dog does.*

The Other End Of The Leash

Leash laws are like speed limits - everyone seems to have a private interpretation of their validity. Some dog owners never go outside with an unleashed dog; others treat the laws as suggestions or disregard them completely. It is not the purpose of this book to tell dog owners where to go to evade the leash laws or reveal the parks where rangers will look the other way at an unleashed dog. Nor is it the business of this book to preach vigilant adherence to the leash laws. Nothing written in a book is going to change people's behavior with regard to leash laws. So this will be the last time leash laws are mentioned, save occasionally when we point out the parks where dogs are welcomed off leash.

Visiting Connecticut Parks

A couple of notes before heading out to the park with your dog. The State of Connecticut has embraced the Internet age and encourages park visitors to print out maps from their website before arriving. Finding a map on site has become increasingly rare and even though these are day hikes, nothing ruins a day out with your dog like getting lost when you don't want to. If you can't pre-print maps on your home computer make a habit of keeping a notebook in the car so you can sketch a map from the information boards found at most parks.

Many public lands in Connecticut allow hunting. If you can only hike with your dog in such places during hunting season, outfit yourself and your dog in blaze orange and stick to the trails. There is no hunting anywhere in Connecticut on Sundays so that is obviously the best day to plan an expedition during hunting season.

No Dogs

Before we get started on the best places to take your dog, let's get out of the way some of the trails that do not allow dogs:

Burnham Brook Preserve - East Haddam
Dinosaur State Park (trails) - Rocky Hill
Greenwich Audubon Center - Greenwich
Haley Farm State Park - Groton
Indian Well State Park - Shelton
Lucius Pond Ordway/Devil's Den Preserve - Weston
Selden Preserve - Old Lyme
Sharon Audubon Center - Sharon
Sherwood Island State Park - Westport (April 15 to September 30)
Squantz State Park - New Fairfield (April 15 to September 30)
Weir Nature Preserve - Wilton

O.K. that wasn't too ba. Let's forget about these and move on to some of the great places where we CAN take our dogs on Connecticut trails...

The 57 Best Places To Hike With Your Dog In Connecticut...

1
Steep Rock Reservation

The Park

More than any other architect, Ehrick Rossiter, working in the late 19th century, gave Washington its distinctive look. He designed over 20 buildings in the town, many in a rambling Colonial Revival style. In 1889, just as he was about to break ground on his own country house he discovered that the wooded hillsides that would be his view were slated for clear cutting. Instead of building the house he bought the threatened land from the timber company.

Rossiter caressed his 100 acres for 36 years, building carriage roads and small river crossings. In 1925 he donated the land, which included the Steep Rock overlook, to a carefully chosen group of trustees, thus ensuring its preservation. Over the years additional landowner donations have swelled the Steep Rock Association's holdings to 4,500+ acres.

The Walks

Attractive woodlands, a sporty trail, a one-of-a-kind view, a long riverside ramble - Steep Rock Reservation has it all for your dog. The *Steep Rock Loop* leaves from the west side of the Shepaug River on a wide, switchbacking path into the hills. When the hemlocks give way to hardwoods the path gets rockier but is still easy on the paw.

Litchfield

Phone Number
- (860) 868-9131

Website
- www.steeprockassoc.org

Admission Fee
- None

Park Hours
- Sunrise to sunset

Directions
- *Washington Depot*; from Route 47 in town, turn down River Road on the west side of the Shepaug River. In a mile, when the road turns right, bear left onto the wide dirt Tunnel Road. Parking is on both sides of the river.

An avenue of massive, multi-trunked Eastern hemlock trees give your dog a special place to rest.

Bonus

The Shepaug Valley Railroad began operation in 1872, bringing vacationers up from New York City.
The Holiday House was a rambling hotel built in 1893 as a retreat for young working women. To reach the resort the trunk line required a tunnel to be blasted 238 feet through solid rock, barely wider than the tracks themselves. The Steep Rock trails use the railbed which ceased operation in 1948, including a walk through the craggy tunnel.

The destination is the overlook of the Clam Shell, where the river loops back on itself. Your dog can stay well back of the fence and soak in the dramatic view from a rock outcropping.

Heading back down the wooded slopes, you'll be using carriage roads, passing through a striking series of multi-trunked hemlocks. At the river your dog will cross on the Hauser Footbridge, a cable-and-wood suspension bridge in the fashion of the Brooklyn Bridge.

The last half of this 4.2-mile loop follows the old rail bed along the Shepaug River. There is plenty of opportunity for your dog to slip in for a swim on this easy stretch. There are more trails that hug the tranquil river and elsewhere in the hills to extend your dog's hiking day in this magical place.

Trail Sense: The mapboard is on the west side of the river even though the main parking lot is on the east side. The main trails are blazed but be careful at the intersections.

Dog Friendliness
Dogs are allowed to hike around the Steep Rock Reservation.
Traffic
Bikes are not permitted but horses are.
Canine Swimming
The beautiful Shepaug River is just deep enough for joyful dog paddling.
Trail Time
Less than an hour for an easy walk along the river to several hours in the Steep Rock hills.

2
Sleeping Giant State Park

The Park

Most of the basaltic ridges in Connecticut run predictably from north to south but one rogue two-mile band of hills runs east-west. The ridge is easily recognized, especially from the original settlements on the southern coast, even more so because the ridge resembles a giant man resting on his back.

American Indians shied away from the ridge, considering it an evil spirit. Early settlers did some milling here but its history has been mostly for recreation. Summer cottages were common on the ridgetops beginning in the mid 1800s.

One of those cottages belonged to Willis Cook, who had started work in a Mt. Carmel axle shop at the age of 10 and in forty years of time came to own the business. He was appointed postmaster and a Hamden judge. He owned the ridge that formed the Giant's head. Dismayed by vandalism, he leased his land for quarrying the mountain's traprock. As blasting began to transform the Giant's silhouette, horrified residents began laying the foundation for the Sleeping Giant Park Association.

New Haven

Phone Number
- (203) 789-7498

Website
- www.ct.gov/dep/cwp/view. asp?a=2716&q=325264&depN av_GID=1650#map

Admission Fee
- None except seasonally on the weekends and holidays

Park Hours
- 8:00 a.m. to sunset

Directions
- *Hamden*; across from Quinnipiac University on Mt. Carmel Avenue. From I-91 take Exit 10 to Route 40 to Route 10 North and turn right on Mt. Carmel. From I-84 take Route 70 South to Route 10 South and left on Mt. Carmel.

The Walks

Just about any kind of canine hiking fare is on the menu in this cherished park. There are more than 30 miles of trails running from the feet to the head of the Giant, the first trails in Connecticut to be designated a National Recreation Trail. Most are rocky and tricky but even the novice trail dog can tackle the gently ascending road that makes up the 1.6-mile *Tower Path*. Your destination on top of the 739-foot Mount Carmel summit is a hulking four-story stone observation tower that would not be out of place in King Arthur's time. Experienced dogs can reach the tower, located near the hip of the Giant, via the difficult *Blue Trail*.

The wooded ridges obscure the rocky nature of the ground. Many of the ascents are pick-your-way passages. At some spots around cobbles of jumbled boulders like Hezekiah's Knob the trail narrows enough to demand care with your dog. Even the *Nature Trail* involves some rough going a ways into it. This detailed, one-hour exploration is a stand-out of its kind, offering an excellent background to your visit to the Giant.

Trail Sense: There is quite a tangle of trails visiting every body part of the Giant. Pick a destination, plot a course from the trailhead kiosks and set out.

Dog Friendliness
Dogs are allowed throughout the state park and forest.

Traffic
Head down some of the more challenging trails and you can find long stretches of solitude; on some of the less steep paths you may see a horse or two so keep your dog close.

Canine Swimming
Water is not the attraction here; the small ponds tend to be swampy.

Trail Time
Plan to spend the day with your dog enjoying these trails.

3
Bluff Point
Coastal Reserve

The Park

Bluff Point is the last remaining undeveloped public land of any size along the Connecticut coastline. That is an irony since it was one of the first to be developed.

Connecticut Governor John Winthrop (1698-1707), grandson of the founding governor of the Massachusetts Bay Colony, made his home on the peninsula and subsequent generations farmed the land for more than a century.

Over the years more than 100 vacation homes were built around the headlands of Bluff Point. Each and every cottage was destroyed during the Hurricane of 1938 and none was rebuilt.

New London

Phone Number
- (860) 444-7591

Website
- www.ct.gov/dep/cwp/view.asp?a=2716&q=325178

Admission Fee
- None

Park Hours
- 8:00 a.m. to sunset

Directions
- *Groton*; Take Exit 88 from I-95 onto Route 117 South to Route 1 South. Turn right and make a left at the first light onto Depot Road. Follow to the end, bearing right under the railroad underpass into the large parking lot.

The State had eyed the bluff as a possible recreation site since before World War I but the first land here was not acquired until 1963. In 1975 Bluff Point was designated a "Coastal Reserve" to preserve its unique ecological integrity.

The Walks

Most of your dog's trotting around Bluff Point will take place on a wide, level cart road that serviced the long-gone agricultural fields. The trip from the parking lot to Bluff Point in the Long Island Sound is 1.6 miles through alternating maritime forest and open shore land. Easy grades take you up to your ultimate destination atop the pink granite rocks of the bluff.

A short detour leads to a one-mile wide sand spit that connects to the small Bushy Point Beach. Your dog will salivate at the chance to romp across the open sand but it is closed to dogs during the plover nesting season from April 15 to September 15.

The loop back travels along a forested ridge. The highlight on this trail segment are stone ruins of the 300-year old Winthrop homestead.

There are more nooks and crannies to explore on Bluff Point, including a cut-off to the full 3.6-mile loop.

Expect your dog to join the fun shell fishing in the sheltered Poquonnock River.

A side trail wanders along the Providence & Worcester Railroad from the parking lot to Mumford Cove. This trail reaches Haley Farm State Park in about one mile but dogs are not allowed in that park.

Trail Sense: Map boards guide the way both at the parking lot and at Bluff Point before you head back.

Dog Friendliness
Dogs are allowed everywhere except Bushy Point Beach 4/15 to 9/15.
Traffic
Regular trail users take advantage of this seaside hike, including bikes and the occasional horse but nothing keeps a beach crowd down like a one-mile walk to the surf. No motor vehicles are allowed.
Canine Swimming
There is plenty of easy access to superior dog paddling in the Poquonnock River.
Trail Time
More than one hour.

4
Bear Mountain

The Park

Through much of the 19th century reference books stated confidently that no part of Connecticut was higher than 1,000 feet. No one living in the remote Litchfield Hills probably paid what was printed in books much mind but Robbins Battell of the prominent musical family of Norfolk wanted to set the record straight.

He identified Bear Mountain as the highest point in the state, negotiated a long-term lease on the property and had it surveyed to make it official. But having set out in his quest for accuracy, Battell actually muddied the waters more. Long after the expert flutist, state senator and philanthropist died in 1894 modern surveying techniques identified the side of Mount Frissell, four miles away, as the highest point in Connecticut. Bear Mountain, however, is the state's highest summit.

Litchfield

Phone Number
- None

Website
- None

Admission Fee
- None

Park Hours
- Sunrise to sunset

Directions
- *Salisbury*; head north on Route 41 from the intersection with Route 44 in town. Go 3.5 miles to a large parking lot on the left for the *Undermountain Trail* (it is signed).

The Walks

Every Nutmeg state dog should get a chance to stand on the state's highest summit. The most popular route is via the blue-blazed *Undermountain Trail* to the *Appalachian Trail*, tagging the peak in just under three miles. Bear Mountain is an honest mountain - there is scarcely a downhill step on the ascent to the top - no depressing drops into saddles and ravines that set tails to drooping when you know you should be headed up. You are gaining over 1,500 feet in elevation on this canine hike but the serious panting does not begin until the final half-mile.

Across Bear Mountain you'll find view-blocking stretches of blueberry and huckleberry struggling with pitch pines and oaks in the stingy mountaintop soils. The views come soon enough, first to the west, then to the south and finally in all directions.

You can continue across the summit and return on the 2.1-mile *Paradise Lane Trail* that crosses upland forests with small ups and downs. The drop down the north slope is steep, quick and rocky and will challenge the most cautious of dogs so take your time here. The full loop with a backtrack on the *Undermountain Trail* will cover about 6.6 miles.

After climbing to the state's highest peak your dog has earned a rest.

Trail Sense: After studying the map on the information board, the blazes will be sufficient to get you to the top and back.

Dog Friendliness
Dogs are welcome on these mountain trails.
Traffic
Foot traffic only and you can expect to see other hikers any time of the year. Some weekends it can seem like a parade.
Canine Swimming
Seasonal streams and a vernal pond are the best you can hope for.
Trail Time
About half a day.

5
Macedonia Brook State Park

The Park

The Scatacook Indians were the first to settle in the hills around the confluence of the Housatonic and Ten Mile rivers. Not much changed when the British founded Kent in 1738. In fact, when the American Revolution broke out in 1775, Scatacook volunteers operated a signal system up on the ridgetops.

The valley around Macedonia evolved into an important early American iron center. Every tree for miles around was cut to fee the hungry forges of the Kent Iron Company. By 1848 there were none left. Not that it mattered since more productive iron mines were putting eastern forges out of business. Kent survived to the end of the Civil War before its forge went cold.

Litchfield

Phone Number
- (860) 927-3238

Website
- www.ct.gov/dep/cwp/view.asp?a=2716&q=325234&depNav_GID=1650

Admission Fee
- None

Park Hours
- 8:00 a.m. to sunset

Directions
- *Kent*; from Route 7 in the center of town take Route 341 west to Macedonia Brook Road. Turn right and stay left to the park.

The core lands for the state park came to Connecticut in 1918 from siblings Alain and May White, dispersing a family fortune made when Danbury was the fur hat capital of the world. Federal Conservation Corps workers during the Great Depression of the 1930s reforested and built the park.

The Walks

Any level of canine hiker will delight in Macedonia Brook State Park. Dogs looking for a ramble down a shady country lane can set out on dirt roads and grassy paths that run along and across Macedonia Brook. You can spend over an hour hiking in the valley and past the campground.

The prize for adventurous dogs is Cobble Mountain with its splendid vews to the west across the Hudson River to the Catskill Mountains. From the center of the park a short, rugged boulder scramble - maybe the state's harshest - leads to the Cobble Mountain summit. If your dog can't make it or you can't lift him, retreat and access the blue-blazed _Macedonia Ridge Trail_ that circles the park. This spirited route covers more than six miles and crosses four hilltops in a very rewarding circuit but can be shortened with connector trails if you notice your dog flagging.

Trail Sense: The trails are well-marked and signed.

Kent Falls make a worthy sidetrip for your dog when visiting Macedonia State Park.

Dog Friendliness

Dogs are allowed to hike the park trails and snack in the sreamside picnic areas but can not stay in the campground.

Traffic

Up on the peaks surrounding the valley the trail will likely be yours; you can expect a mountain biker or two.

Canine Swimming

Don't bother the fly fishermen and your dog can cool off in Macedonia Brook.

Trail Time

More than one hour.

6
Devil's Hopyard State Park

The Park

No one knows the definitive origin of this park's colorful name. Several eerie tales involve the supernatural but the real story may just be that a farmer named Dibble once grew hops for brewing beer in a field here.

The centerpiece of the park is Chapman Falls that spills in cascades down layers of erosion-resistant schist. The falls powered mills during the 1800s and logging continued in the area until 1919 when Miss A.G. Willard of Colchester convinced the State Park and Forest Commission to purchase 860 acres through the Eight Mile River valley and stop the logging.

Middlesex

Phone Number
- (860) 873-8566

Website
- www.ct.gov/dep/cwp/view.asp?a=2716&q=325188

Admission Fee
- None

Park Hours
- Sunrise to sunset

Directions
- *East Haddam*; off of Route 82, east of the Connecticut River. Follow signs to the park along Hopyard Road.

The Walks

Devil's Hopyard is one of the best places to take your dog hiking in central Connecticut. You'll find 15 miles of trails with the star being the 2.5-mile, orange-blazed *Vista Trail*. Starting across a covered bridge the route alternates between a pick-your-way trail through the rocks and a wide and inviting path under an open hemlock forest. After skirting the cold-water Eight Mile River the trail climbs briskly up the hillside to an overlook of the valley. The loop crosses the higher elevations of the park before finishing at Chapman Falls.

One of the highlights of the park is the Devils Oven, a rock formation that can be explored via a short trail that is nearly vertical. Your dog's four-wheel drive will be an asset on this path but it is heavily littered with glass so unless you are a major fan of glacial rock carvings, just observe from below.

Trail Sense: The trails are well-blazed and junctions are marked with distance and direction by signposts.

Dog Friendliness

Dogs are allowed on trails and picnic areas but not in the campground.

Traffic

Bikes can use some of the trails on the west side of Hopyard Road.

Canine Swimming

There is easy access to Eight Mile River along the *Vista Trail*, including a small, pebbly beach just downstream from Chapman Falls.

Trail Time

Several hours or more.

Multi-tiered Chapman Falls is the great attraction of Devil's Hopyard.

7
Burr Pond
State Park

The Park

In 1851, Milo Burr built a rock dam at the meeting of several mountain streams to create a lake whose water powered local industries. Every tree of any size was eventually chopped down to feed a tannery and three sawmills.

Now, 150 years later, Burr Pond looks like a natural mountain lake rimmed with boulders and speckled with small islands. The trees are back, too.

The Walks

The canine hike around Burr Pond is the best circumnavigation of a lake in Connecticut. The footpath, actually built by Philip Buttrick during the Great Depression for the Civilian Conservation Corps, is almost universally wide, often flat and traverses airy hemlocks and yellow birches. Toss in the occasional brook crossing, impressive rock outcropping, tiny coves and nearly constant glimpses of the water and you have the recipe for a quality day for your dog.

On the opposite shore gentle, rocky inclines begin to intrude which gives you a feel for what awaits on the intersecting *Muir Trail* through the adjoining Paugnut State Forest. Your goal here is 1,326-foot Walnut Mountain, which you will tag and return, adding a couple of hours to your dog's day in the woods.

Trail Sense: The *Red Trail*, blazed in blue of course, is well-marked around Burr Pond. If you are looking for the *Muir Trail* junction, pay attention because it sneaks up on you a bit. A mapboard at the beach will orient you.

Litchfield

Phone Number
- (860) 482-1817

Website
- www.ct.gov/dep/cwp/view.asp?A=2716&Q=325180

Admission Fee
- None except seasonally on the weekends and holidays

Park Hours
- 8:00 a.m. to sunset

Directions
- *Torrington*; from Route 8 take Exit 46 and go west on Pinewoods Road. At the end turn left onto Winsted Road. Turn right at the blinking light to the park uphill on the left.

Dog Friendliness

Dogs are not allowed on the beach but can hike the trails and party in the picnic area.

Traffic

Foot traffic only; if you catch a rare day when it is crowded on the loop around Burr Pond you can find solitude on the _Muir Trail_.

Canine Swimming

Every water-loving dog deserves a swim in the clear waters of Burr Pond; access comes at regular intervals on the trail around the pond.

Trail Time

More than one hour.

It's a dog's life in Burr Pond.

8
Westwoods
Trails

The Park

The first land stewarded by the Guilford Land Conservation Trust was a two-acre slice of salt marsh donated in November, 1965. Other small land gifts followed but in the 1970s the Westwoods, a cherished tract of State and Town woodland came under threat of development and the small band of local conservationists really kicked it into gear. Today, it is the largest town land trust in Connecticut with over 2,500 acres in holdings.

The Walks

The centerpiece of the Guilford Trust properties is the elaborate trail system through the 1,200-acre West-

New Haven

Phone Number
- None

Website
- www.westwoodstrails.org/index.html

Admission Fee
- None

Park Hours
- Daylight hours

Directions
- *Guilford*; several entrances west of town, off Route 1. Take Exit 57 off I-95 and follow Route 1 East (to the left).

woods. Almost 40 miles of marked trails criss-cross the property so you can carve out a hiking loop of an hour or a full day of canine hiking. Your dog can find himself trotting across almost anything under the heavily wooded canopy - cobbles, packed dirt, smooth rock, boardwalk.

The longest Westwoods trail is a only a little over three miles (the *White Square* that trips along Lost Lake, a shallow pond separated from Long Island Sound by the railroad) so you can sample several routes in a day. Much of the original trail system created in 1966 can be hiked on the *Green Triangle Nature Trail* that can be accessed on Dunk Rock Road.

The dominant features of Westwoods are the islands of massive rock formations, each one seemingly larger than the one you just passed. Some of the trails (yellow-blazed usually) lead up and across these hulking blocks of granite and require more thought and care while traversing.

Trail Sense: If possible, stop into the Guilford Town Hall at Park Street on Green and pick up a trail map. If not, a map is posted on information boards at trail entrances. Check for trail closures that can be necessitated by the collapsing hemlock trees. The "Westwoods Chainsaw Brigade" has worked diligently for years to keep the trails clear.

Your dog will enjoy exploring the massive granite rock formations found along the many trails of Westwoods.

Dog Friendliness

Dogs are welcome in the Westwoods.

Traffic

No motorized vehicles but bikes are allowed and horses are permitted on several trails.

Canine Swimming

Swimming is not a prominent feature of hiking for your dog here away from Lost Lake.

Trail Time

Many hours possible.

31

9
Trout Brook Valley
Preserve

The Park

Of the 50 states, only Rhode Island has less public land in open space than Connecticut. With the 20th century drawing to a close, the legislature passed a law setting a state goal of holding at least 10 percent of state land area as open space.

The first target for acquisition was the Trout Brook Valley, owned by the Bridgeport Hydraulic Company and slated for conversion into a golf course and housing development. Actor and activist Paul Newman threw his considerable presence and a half-million dollars into saving the valley, spearheading one of the biggest conservation victories Connecticut has seen.

The Aspetuck Land Trust, founded in 1966, has also preserved two adjoining parcels - Crow Hill and Jump Hill - to create a 1000-acre oasis in the middle of one of the most developed areas of New England.

Fairfield

Phone Number
- None

Website
- http://www.aspetuck-landtrust.org/

Admission Fee
- None

Park Hours
- Sunrise to sunset

Directions
- *Weston*; take Exit 44 off the Merritt Parkway, Route 15. Head north on Route 58 and turn left on Route 136. Take the second right onto Old Redding Road. Turn right at the end onto Bradley Lane to the trailhead. You can also park at the end of Elm Drive by going 1.6 miles past Route 136 and turn left onto Freeborn Road. Turn right in .7 of a mile on Elm Drive.

The Walks

Any level of canine hiker will be thrilled as he sets out on the trail descending into the dark hemlock-laced woodlands of Trout Brook Valley. More than 20 miles of well-defined trails lie ahead. As the narrowish footpaths and occasional fire road criss-cross frequently there is ample opportunity to improvise your dog's day and stay out shorter - or longer - in the Preserve.

Experienced canine hikers will want to craft a north-south loop around the property that will last several hours. Your dog will bound into and out of countless ravines and even pick-up a workout up steep ridges. The sportiest hiking with your dog comes down the *Red Trail* along the Saugatuck Reservoir. Despite the rocky stretches the going is usually paw-friendly, even squishy in spots. And what dog doesn't love muddy paws?

Trail Sense: Maps can be had at the trailheads plus the trails are well-marked and "You Are Here" signs are posted at trail junctions.

Dog Friendliness
Dogs are allowed to enjoy Trout Brook Valley.

Traffic
There are trails designated for bike and equestrian use but trail traffic is typically not a concern in the Preserve. Motorized vehicles are not permitted but hunting is allowed.

Canine Swimming
No swimming allowed in Saugatuck Rservoir; the streams are best for splashing.

Trail Time

10
White Memorial Conservation Center

The Park

Alain White and his sister May, heirs to a fur hat fortune, became ardent conservationists at an early age, quietly buying up abandoned farms and logged out mountains in the early 20th century. In 1913, to mark the 50th anniversary of their family coming to Litchfield, they formed a non-profit foundation in their parents' memory.

Much of the land the Whites donated became Connecticut state parks and forests. Around their ancestral home of Whitehall evolved the 4,000 acres of the White Memorial Conservation Center. Knowing the towns could not afford to lose the taxes on the land, the White Memorial Foundation became and still is a voluntary taxpayer.

Litchfield

Phone Number
- (860) 567-0857

Website
- www.whitememorialcc.org/

Admission Fee
- None

Park Hours
- Sunrise to sunset

Directions
- *Litchfield*; west of town on Route 202. From the junction of Route 202 and Route 63 go two miles west to the sign at Bissell Road on the left. Make the immediate right onto Whitehall Road to the parking lot in the office/museum area.

The Walks

Whatever your dog likes in an outing on the trail can be found here on the Center's cornucopia of footpaths. Enjoy long, easy walks through mixed woodlands? Follow the *Pine Island Trail* across Bissell Road or the *Interpretive Trail* under big trees out of the museum parking lot. Does your dog look forward to the open spaces and sensory salad of wetlands? Boardwalks bring access to Duck Pond and Little Pond. Want traditional northwest Connecticut canine hiking through boulder-studded hills? There is plenty of that here as well.

There are 25 named trails, most less than one mile, and probably as many unnamed trails across White Memorial. Study the detailed property map in the parking lot pavilion to plan your day with your dog. The trails are dissected by active roads so expect to walk your dog into potential traffic at some point. Out on the trails she will be trotting along anything from soft grass to gravel roads.

Trail Sense: Accessing the trailheads will be your biggest challenge. Everything is well-marked but there are so many side trails that it is easy to wander down an unexpected path.

Handy boardwalks take your dog into the deep recesses of the wetlands in White Memorial.

Dog Friendliness

Dogs are allowed throughout the reserve and in the campground.

Traffic

Bicycles and horses are allowed on selected trails but you can seek out quiet trails with your dog with little difficulty.

Canine Swimming

Bantam Lake, the largest natural lake in Connecticut, can be accessed at several points near the campground around Folly's Point.

Trail Time

An hour to a full day.

11
Chatfield Hollow
State Park

The Park

In 1639 three brothers, Francis, Thomas and George Chatfield emigrated from Pagham in the south of England to the wilds of Connecticut. The Chatfields settled in Guilford and their descendants are believed to have worked a gristmill on the Chatfield Hollow brook, that drops to the Long Island Sound through a pair of parallel ridges here.

In 1934, Franklin Roosevelt's "Tree Army," the Civilian Conservation Corps, came to the hollow and built a stone and earth dam across the stream. Schreeder Pond then became the centerpiece of the recreational facilities in the state park.

Middlesex

Phone Number
- (860) 424-3200

Website
- www.ct.gov/dep/cwp/view.
asp?A=2716&Q=325182

Admission Fee
- None except seasonally on the weekends and holidays

Park Hours
- 8:00 a.m. to sunset

Directions
- *Killingworth*; From I-95 take Exit 63 and follow Route 81 north to Route 80 west. The park entrance is on the right.

The Walks

Chatfield Hollow is a good place to bring an adventurous dog with sporty hiking to be had on the both the east and west crests of the park. In fact, there is so much hard, light-colored granitic-type rock called Monson Gneiss scattered about the grounds that some trail sections aren't suitable for dogs. The Indian Caves on the green-blazed *Chimney Trail* require climbs and jumps that most dogs can't make.

Similarly, the going is tough for dogs on the *West Crest Trail*, less so across the light woods and thin soils of the connecting *Lookout Trail* and *Ridge Trail* on the East Crest. Even the flat going on the *Covered Bridge Trail* can be a challenge with its abundance of rocks and exposed tree roots. But the trail segments are short and the entrance road can be used to close loops so if your dog isn't enjoying the hiking you can cut short your explorations. Many dog

The open-latticed covered bridge in Chatfield Hollow.

walkers simply use the 1.1-mile serpentine entrance road for their dog's outing at Chatfield Hollow.

If your dog is just getting warmed up on these short, rugged jaunts, however, you can head east and follow the *Chatfield Trail* into the Cockaponset State Forest. Here you can experience more of the handiwork of glaciers that scraped and pushed the rocks around 10,000 years ago.

Trail Sense: The trails are well-blazed and color-coded.

Dog Friendliness
Dogs are allowed on the trails and there are plenty of poop bags available along the entrance road.

Traffic
This is a popular park but only the hardy get deep into the trails.

Canine Swimming
Dogs are not allowed in the swimming ponds; Chatfield Hollow Brook is a rocky stream with a few, but not many, pools.

Trail Time
More than one hour.

12
Pachaug
State Forest

The Park

Indians of the Narragansett, Pequot, and Mohegan tribes hunted along the Pachaug River (the name "Pachaug" means "bend int he river") for centuries. In the late 1700s British colonists, with the help of the Mohegans, began skirmishing with the local Indians. When the Narragansetts and Pequots were defeated a six mile square tract was granted to the Indian War Veterans. Eventually, the central portion of this land grant became "Volunteer's Town," incorporated as Voluntown in 1721.

The first land for the Pachaug State Forest was purchased in 1928. On June 6, 1933 Camp Lonergan, one of the first Civilian Conservation Corps work camps, was established here to develop recreational facilites. Today Pachaug covers about 24,000 acres in six towns, and is the largest state forest in Connecticut.

New London

Phone Number
- (860) 376-4075

Website
- www.ct.gov/dep/cwp/view.asp?a=2716&q=325068&depNav_GID=1650

Admission Fee
- None except seasonally on the weekends and holidays

Park Hours
- 8:00 a.m. to sunset

Directions
- *Voluntown*; take I-395 south, Exit 85 onto Route 138 East. Follow for 9 miles and take a left onto Route 49 north to the entrance on the left. For the Green Falls Area take Route 138 east for 8.3 miles to the forest entrance.

The Walks

A quartet of long-distance hiking trails traverse this vast public recreation mecca in southeastern Connecticut. Access is from two developed areas, Chapman and Green Falls. At Chapman your dog can indulge in a botanical walk and a little mountain climbing. The trek to the top of 441-foot Mt. Misery, named by settlers dispirited by the abundance of rocks in the soil, can be slick for your dog on exposed rock. The view from the highest point in the vicinity is one-directional but the flat rocks make a fine resting spot with your dog.

One of the most unique canine hikes in Connecticut is the easy stroll through blankets of ferns, Eastern hemlock and Atlantic white cedar in the Rhododendron Sanctuary. A crushed gravel and boardwalk path leads into swampland where you are immersed in magnificent thickets of native rosebay rhododendrons over ten feet tall. Come to the 26-acre sanctuary off the main Chapman parking lot in late spring and early summer to see the plants in full bloom.

For a longer canine hiking day at Chapman, head north along the network of dirt roads or the *Pachaug Trail* to Philips Pond and, further on, to Hell Hollow, a low-lying swampy pond. This is fairly easy going for your dog, completely in forest through interspersed rocky passages.

At Green Falls there are two distinct hikes of interest for your dog. If you come in spring you will certainly want to spin around the 3-mile *Laurel Loop* and lose yourself in the delicate white blossoms of mountain laurel. In the other direction, the *Nehantic Trail* leads to the clear waters of Green Falls Pond, which you can circle with good access for your dog. You will see plenty of stone souvenirs in the form of cellar holes, mill ruins and fences around the pond.

Trail Sense: The main trails are blazed but there are many others, including miles of dirt roads, that are not. A map is mandatory for any serious exploration of Pachaug State Forest.

Dog Friendliness
Dogs are allowed to hike the trails but not stay in the campground.
Traffic
If it moves, you could see it on the forest trails and roads but you can hike for hours in private with your dog away from the recreation areas.
Canine Swimming
Several brooks provide a refreshing splash for your dog and you can reach swimming ponds on the trails.
Trail Time
Many hours to a full weekend.

13

Mount Frissell

The Park

It did not take long for members of the Massachusetts Bay Colony to start migrating inland and by 1642 so many settlers had come to the Connecticut River at Springfield and Hartford that Massachusetts hired surveyors to create a boundary based on its charter: "all the lands to the Pacific Ocean from a point three miles south of the most southerly branch of the Charles River." That border line would be in dispute for the next 164 years and when it was finalized the summit of Mount Frissell wound up jussssssst that far on the Massachusetts side of the line, leaving the highest point in Connecticut on the side of the mountain. And so the Nutmeg State is the only one of the 50 states whose highpoint is not a summit.

Litchfield

Phone Number
- (413) 528-0330

Website
- www.mass.gov/dcr/parks/western/wnds.htm

Admission Fee
- None

Park Hours
- Sunrise to sunset

Directions
- *Salisbury*; take Mt. Riga Road that becomes Mount Washington Road. Go north into Massachusetts and continue as it becomes East Street. The parking area for the Forest Headquarters is on the left.

The Walks

There are several options for your dog to stand at the highest point in Connecticut. The most direct is from the trailhead on East Street that takes you up and over Round Mountain and onto Mount Frissell in a little over a mile. The climbs are steady but won't overwhelm a healthy trail dog. A little ways past the roof of Connecticut and 80 feet higher is the open, grassy summit that has been heretofore obscured by the thick trees.

If your goal is simply to tag the highest point in the state, turn around and head back. but as long as you're up here... The marquee canine hike in Mount Washington State Forest is the trek to 2240-foot Alander Mountain and its expansive 270-degree views that may be the best in western Massachusetts.

After passing the Tri-State Marker you can head north on the lightly traveled *Ashley Hill Trail* through lush forests and head back up to Alander Mountain.

Until the campground about halfway back to the summit the going is on a wide jeep road and there will be plenty of unbridged stream crossings that your dog will happily bound through.

Your dog can't get this view of Campbell Falls in Massachusetts without hiking through Connecticut.

When your dog gets his fill of mountaintop views of the Hudson Valley and the Catskills continue across to the *South Taconic Trail* to close your loop. If you plan to make the big loop you can also start your day in the forest headquarters and just take a jog down the *Mount Frissell Trail*, rather than cross Round Mountain. The loop over Alander Mountain will cover about eleven miles.

Trail Sense: All these trails are well-blazed but get a map.

Dog Friendliness
Dogs are allowed to tag these summits.
Traffic
You'll likely be sharing these views with a hiker or two.
Canine Swimming
There are plenty of streams in Washington State Forest, mostly of the splashing variety.
Trail Time
About two hours to reach the Connecticut highpoint and return; a full day to include Alander Mountain.

14
Collis P. Huntington State Park

The Park

Much of this hilltop property was developed in the early 1900s by Walter Lutgen, a business associate of August Belmont. Lutgen built lakes and miles of Victorian carriage roads to emulate the woodland estates of his native Germany.

After going broke during the Great Depression Lutgen lost his estate and it was purchased by Archer Huntington, scion to the empire built by Transcontinental Railroad pioneer Collis P. Huntington, for whom the park was named. Archer Huntington was a scholar with wide-ranging interests. He was the nation's leading authority on all things Spanish and helped found nearly 20 museums and wildlife preserves around the country. Huntington called his estate Stanerigg, for the Scottish word for "stony ridge," and it was his last home. The state park opened after his wife's death in 1973.

Fairfield

Phone Number
- (860) 242-1158

Website
- www.ct.gov/dep/cwp/view.asp?a=2716&q=325222&depNav_GID=1650

Admission Fee
- None

Park Hours
- 8:00 a.m. to sunset

Directions
- *Redding*; on Sunset Hill Road off Route 58, 10 miles north of Route 15, the Merritt Parkway and 4.6 miles south of Route 302. The first entrance on the right is the larger parking lot next to the town's Couch Hill Preserve. Year-round trailhead parking is down the way at Dodgingtown Road.

The Walks

Your dog is in for several distinct canine hiking experiences at the old Huntington place. Most of your trail time will cover the wide, old carriage roads across the wooded bumps and hogbacks. These country lane rambles with your dog can cover miles.

The white-blazed trip above Lake Hopewell that twists vigorously through rock formations was designed by mountain bikers but is great fun for your dog as he slaloms along. It is a fast-paced one-mile journey that is remark-ablypaw-friendly in between the rocks and roots.

South of the lake your dog can enjoy the relatively rare Connecticut experience of beautiful open fields and athletic dogs can also access the long-distance *Aspetuck Valley Trail* in Huntington State Park.

Anna Huntington's family of howling wolves stand at the park entrance.

Trail Sense: Maps are available and there are just enough markings on the trail to inspire confidence. Look hard for trail junctions, however.

Dog Friendliness
Dogs are welcome to hike in the park.
Traffic
Bikes are allowed but this is not a busy park - there is nothing to do but use the trails.
Canine Swimming
Although much of the shoreline is mucky there are a couple of good access points in Lake Hopewell - the earthen dam for one. There is good dog paddling in the surrounding lagoons as well.
Trail Time
More than one hour.

15
Lower Paugussett State Forest

The Park

Since the earliest colonial times, the Housatonic River has been used as a source of power. The first dams were built to operate gristmills and sawmills, and later to turn turbines. In 1870 the first dam for the generation of electric power was constructed across the river between Derby and Shelton..

Other hydroelectric power dams were built in Great Barrington, Falls Village, and Kent. Planning for the Stevenson Dam began before 1900 and ground was broken in 1917. When the 122-foot high dam was completed two years later the resulting Lake Zoar became the fifth largest freshwater body in the state, flooding deserted dairy farms and remnants of villages with Housatonic water for over ten miles.

Fairfield

Phone Number
- None

Website
- None

Admission Fee
- None

Park Hours
- Sunrise to sunset

Directions
- *Stevenson*; take Exit 11 off I-84 to Route 34. Go east (right) for 4.9 miles and make a left on Great Quarter Road to parking area at end.

The Walks

Setting out on the blue-blazed *Lake Zoar Trail* the destination for most canine hikers is the cascading Prydden Falls, a few tail wags past 1.5 miles away. To get there your dog won't trot on a more agreeable trail in all of Connecticut. Traversing an open hemlock forest, the footpath/woods road bounces over of

44

bounces and rolls along the hillside. The path is smooth enough that you won't take a tumble if you get distracted by the spectacular views of Lake Zoar.

When you reach Prydden Brook a small, unmarked trail leads to the falls on the right (look for a sign posted on a tree for confirmation). It is a seasonal falls so in late summer there may not be enough water for your dog to refresh in the sluices and pools as the water makes it way 100 feet down to the lake.

This will be as far as it goes for most canine hikers and you will retrace your pawprints back to the trailhead. But you can venture further up the lakeshore before turning back (heed the trail detour from April 15 to August 15 for nesting birds) or even head up into the hills for a six-mile loop. This is a much rougher hike than the opening stretch to the falls and you will need to take your dog a half-mile down a narrow, albeit lightly used, residential road to return to the your vehicle.

Trail Sense: A mapboard at the trailhead will help acquaint you with the forest and the route is well-blazed in blue and yellow.

Dog Friendliness
Dogs are allowed to hike in the state forest.
Traffic
You may encounter other trail users early in the hike but solitude is your likely reward for taking your dog deeper into the forest.
Canine Swimming
Absolutely - in Lake Zoar.
Trail Time
From two to four hours.

16
Ragged Mountain Preserve

The Park

Hikers have been making their way to the top of the exposed cliffs on Ragged Mountain for as long as there have been people in Connecticut. Although closely flanked by residential neighborhoods, today the mountain has been laced with conservation easements that should keep it open for years to come.

The Walks

When you study a map before tackling Ragged Mountain you notice that you will be hiking about two miles to reach the 761-foot summit. Taking into account your trailhead elevation of 230 feet and doing some quick ciphering, it

Hartford

Phone Number
- None

Website
- None

Admission Fee
- None

Park Hours
- Dusk to dawn

Directions
- *Berlin*; south of town via Route 71A. Turn west on Wigwam Road and park on the right where it ends at West Lane.

can be easy to conclude an easy day on the mountain waits. But soon your dog is bounding into and out of numerous ravines and you realize that you are indeed in for a workout on Ragged Mountain.

The 50+ mile *Metacomet Trail* is the most celebrated of the many footpaths and old roads you can find in the preserve and most canine hikers will combine that blue-blazed route with the *Ragged Mountain Preserve Trail* to fashion a hiking loop of just under seven miles. Take care with your dog when you reach the exposed cliffs - there is plenty of room to maneuver but it is not the place for a rambunctious dog.

The trail trips along the cliff edges for a good distance, ducking into the woods every now and then. On the mountain are plenty of rocky pawfalls but the open woodland offers wiggle room for your dog as you move along.

Trail Sense: Study the map at the trailhead. The trails are generally well-blazed but the route doesn't always go in the obvious direction so pay attention and don't go too far without seeing a colored blaze.

On top of Ragged Mountain you aren't so high that you still can't hear barking dogs from the neighborhoods below.

Dog Friendliness
Dogs are allowed on Ragged Mountain.

Traffic
Parking is limited but what is available is often taken; foot traffic only.

Canine Swimming
No swimming on Ragged Mountain, although a seasonal stream may be flowing.

Trail Time
Expect three to four hours to complete the circuit to the summit and back.

17
Barn Island Wildlife Management Area

The Park

In the 1930s the Barn Island Marshes, like most of the wetlands in New England, were ditched for mosquito control. In the late 1940s, the Connecticut Board of Fisheries and Game began constructing a series of impoundments across the valley marshes to offset the loss of waterfowl habitat caused by the mosquito ditching.

Low earthen dikes converted the wetlands into non-tidal, shallow water habitat that indeed attracted more waterfowl but by the 1970s the impoundments were dominated by Narrow-leaved Cattail and expanding colonies of Phragmites. Restoration of tidal flushing was accomplished by reconfiguring the culverts.

Today the actively managed 1,013-acre Barn Island Marshes are the State's single largest coastal property.

The Walks

Four impoundments have created

New London

Phone Number
- None

Website
- www.lisrc.uconn.edu/coasta-laccess/site.asp

Admission Fee
- None

Park Hours
- Sunrise to sunset

Directions
- *Stonington*; Take Exit 91 from I-95 to Route 234/Pequot Trail. Turn left onto North Main Street and continue to Route 1/Stonington-Westerly Road. Turn left onto and right onto Greenhaven Road after crossing Wequetequock Cove. Make an immediate right onto Palmer Neck Road for 1.4 miles to a parking area on the right before boat launch area. The trail is across the road.

islands of woodlands typical of upstate Connecticut along the shores of Wequetequock Cove. Four miles of trails wander across the dikes and down old farm roads, alternating between open salt-water marsh hiking and more familiar woods walking. As you go, look for remnants of the farming heritage of the site - stone walls that once lined cropland are now in the marsh, evidence of the rise in sea level over the centuries.

This is easy trotting for your dog with only gentle elevation changes across Barn Island. Expect some of the trails to be overgrown in summer, however. Barn Island is an active hunting area after September 1 so dress yourself and your dog in blaze orange until March.

Trail Sense: An information board and map are located across the first dike for orientation but nothing is marked out on the trail.

Dog Friendliness
Dogs are welcome to hike here.

Traffic
Barn Island is popular with birders in the cooler months but the trails are seldom crowded.

Canine Swimming
There is open water for a doggie dip at the boat launch which is a short walk from the parking area.

Trail Time
More than an hour is possible.

18
Hubbard
Park

The Park

When volcanoes stopped rumbling and spewing lava about 200 million years ago the entire region cooled, fractured and tilted to the west leaving the East Peak/West Peak that is reportedly the highest mountain within 25 miles of the coastline from Cadillac Mountain in Maine to Florida.

Walter Hubbard, whose ancestors landed on these shores in 1633, lived a classic 19th century American success story: grow up on a farm, start work early as a store clerk, save and dream, open your own store at age 30, see an opportunity with the discovery of kerosene, start a company that becomes the world leader in lamps, evolve into civic leader.

At the age of 76 Hubbard, drawing on his many trips to Europe, imported Italian stonemasons to build a 32-foot cylindrical medieval tower on land he owned atop East Peak overlooking Meriden. The 32-foot high Castle Craig was dedicated with much fanfare on October 29, 1900. Hubbard then donated land for a surrounding park, consulting on its design with the Olmstead Brothers, sons of Frederick Law Olmstead of Central Park fame.

Litchfield

Phone Number
- (203) 630-4259

Website
- www.cityofmeriden.org/CMS/
default.asp?CMS_PageID=426

Admission Fee
- None

Park Hours
- Sunrise to sunset

Directions
- *Meriden*; for the *Metacomet Trail* take Exit 5 off I-691 Eastbound and go north on Route 71 to pull-offs past Kensington Avenue. The main entrance to the park is further north at Park Drive off Butler Street.

The Walks

The Hanging Hills are full of steep hiking trails and beautiful, scenic views for your dog. The prime destination for most visitors will be Castle Craig, reached by the *Metacomet Trail*. The climb to the traprock tower above Merimere Reservoir is more challenging for the rock scrambling under paw than for the taxing climb so take your time and enjoy the views as you go. This is an out-and-back canine hike so you will return the way you came.

There is much else for your dog to do in the 1,800-acre park as well. Dozens of unmarked wooded trails in the Hanging Hills and grassy fields begging for a game of fetch in the developed section of the Hubbard Park, for instance.

Trail Sense: Blue blazes will lead you to Castle Craig; the adventure begins if you take your dog off the main route.

Dog Friendliness

Dogs are allowed to hike these trails.

Traffic

Bikes are allowed on park trails; a road leads to Castle Craig so you will meet more folks at the end of your hike than on the way.

Canine Swimming

The Elmere Reservoir and Merimere Reservoir are off-limits and Mirror Lake is more for admiring fountains than swimming dogs.

Trail Time

Several hours.

19

Housatonic Meadows State Park

The Park

Industry came early to the Sharon Valley along the Housatonic River. The area prospered as one of America's most important early mining and refining centers, at one point earning the moniker of "Mousetrap Capital of the World."

Iron production ended in 1925 and a few years later the Civilian Conservation Corps established a camp here to develop this park and other nearby recreation facilities.

The Walks

Housatonic Meadows is cherished today for its piney campground and excellent flyfishing in the chilly waters of the river. Hiking? Not so much. But Housatonic Meadows may be the best single-trail park in the state.

That trail is the *Pine Knob Loop*, a sporty exploration that tops two small peaks through exceedingly pleasing woodland. The loop is actually a melding of three trails, including the *Appalachian Trail*. This attractive trail that covers about 2.5 miles is lure enough to bring your dog but Pine Knob also serves up memorable overlooks of the Housatonic River below. For some reason, if the loop seems too daunting for your dog, you could park at the campground, cross Route 7 and scamper up to an overlook and return.

Trail Sense: As the trail is disconnected from the main park by busy Route 7, your biggest challenge will be safely getting your dog to the trailhead.

Dog Friendliness

Dogs are not allowed in the popular riverside campground but can hike the *Pine Knob Trail* across the road.

Traffic

This is an easy access point for the *Appalachian Trail* so Pine Knob loopers will mingle with the long-distance trekkers.

Canine Swimming

Hatch Brook is a noisy companion along the *Red Trail* where your dog will love splashing in the cascades. With a little determination you can get your water-loving dog into the Housatonic Rver but be careful parking along and crossing Route 7 and its blind curves. Don't disturb the fly fishermen though.

Trail Time

Between one and two hours.

"No one appreciates the very special genius of your conversation as a dog does."

-Christopher Morley

20
Mile of Ledges

The Park

This stretch of the blue-blazed *Tunxis Trail* follows lands and around reservoirs owned by the Bristol Water Department. It is the terminus of the northern section of the trail coming down from Massachusetts.

The Walks

The Mile of Ledges is not the fabrication of some publicist. The trail crawls up and down over boulders, fissures and overhangs for that mile. The rugged, challenging route is one of Connecticut's most celebrated hikes, but chances are your dog wasn't polled.

An athletic dog can make the journey and may even revel in the jumping and challenge in finding a passable route. But this is not the place for an inexperienced tail dog. Many dogs will find the drop-offs and tight passages intimidating. In certain spots - Bear's Den comes to mind - only a Houdini-dog will find his way out. Take your time, look for alternate routes and plan on plenty of cajoling and lifting on this canine hike.

After passing through the Mile of Ledges you won't want to turn around and retrace your steps and luckily you can make a loop by walking a half-mile on lightly traveled Greer Road and return on the *Yellow-Dot Trail*. The toughest part of this northerly route comes at the beginning but your dog will welcome the chance to hike on dirt instead of rock. The full loop, completely under trees, will cover over four miles.

Trail Sense: The trails are well-marked through the boulders. Finding the trailhead for the *Yellow-Dot Trail* on Greer Road is your biggst obstacle to wayfinding. It is tucked in the woods on the left when the road becomes a driveway.

Litchfield
Phone Number - None
Website - None
Admission Fee - None
Park Hours - Dawn to dusk
Directions - *Burlington*; take Route 72 north from Route 6 for 1.7 miles to Preston Road. Go to end at East Plymouth Road and turn left. Parking is at the trailhead along the road in a half-mile.

Shortly after marrying during the American Revolution Stephen Graves, who lived in a cabin near the ledges, was drafted to serve the Colonial Army. He hired a substitute, and while his substitute was still in the service at Grave's expense, he was again drafted. When he protested this injustice, Graves was pursued and arrested as a deserter. He escaped and when he returned home he threw in with many of his neighbors, who were British sympathizers known as Tories. For protection the men worked the area farms together and from time to time took refuge from Colonial troops under the large slabs of granite that came to be known as the Tory Den. Nineteen year-old Mrs. Graves would come at night through "the dark and pathless woods, over rocky ledges" to carry them food. Many efforts were made to find this hiding place, but its location was never known to any but the Tories until after the close of the war.

It looks like another problem to be solved by your dog on the Mile of Ledges.

Dog Friendliness

Dogs are allowed to hike the *Tunxis Trail*.

Traffic

You will find little competition for the trail on this hike.

Canine Swimming

A pond mercilessly appears at the end of the Mile of Ledges. There is too much vegetation for a good swim but your dog will appreciate splashing in the cool waters. Also a small stream is on the stem trail leading to the loop.

Trail Time

Allow at least two hours to complete this loop.

21
Talcott Mountain State Park

The Park

Daniel Wadsworth used the money his father Jeremiah accumulated in Hartford commerce to become one of America's foremost patron of the arts. In 1805 he built one of the country's first mountaintop estates on Talcott Mountain that he called Montevideo. Its most dramatic feature was a 55-foot wooden viewing tower.

Wadsworth was not one to keep views that stretch from Long Island Sound to New Hampshire to himself, however. He freely permitted the public to climb the mountain and use his tower. So many did that the Wadsworth family felt overrun at times. But when the tower blew down in 1840, he built another.

Hartford

Phone Number
- (860) 242-1158

Website
- www.ct.gov/dep/cwp/view.asp?A=2716&Q=325272

Admission Fee
- None except seasonally on the weekends and holidays

Park Hours
- 8:00 a.m. to sunset

Directions
- *Bloomfield*; from Route 202 follow Route 10 North to Route 185. Make a right and the park entrance is on the left at the top of the hill.

In the 1960s Talcott Mountain was slated to be cut up into residential lots when a consortium of private conservationists and public funds mobilized to keep the cherished ridgetop views open to the public.

The Walks

After a brief, spirited climb on an old woods road the *Tower Trail* levels out for the ramble across the ridge to the Heublein Tower. Once off the stony road things improve markedly for your dog's feet on the ridge where the well-worn road turns to dirt. You actually have your choice of two paths most of the time, depending on how close your dog wants to get to the unprotected drop-offs. This road through light woods is wide enough to bring a pack of dogs. The trip to the tower covers about 1.25 miles.

There is more traditional canine hiking on Talbott Mountain as well. The crowds will fade away if you dip behind the rock outcropping with your dog to test these knolls and grades with your dog on the single file *Metacomet Trail*. You can either use this footpath to work your way back down the mountain or combine with the *Old Metacomet Trail* for a 3-mile loop back to the tower.

The kind volunteers in the Hublein Tower put out a ceramic bowl to fill for yoru dog at the top of Talcott Mountain.

Trail Sense: You really can't miss the tower but if you need a map - look on the BACK of the information board.

Dog Friendliness
Dogs are allowed to hike the mountain trails and a ceramic bowl has been left out at the water fountain on the summit for your best trail companion. Dogs are not, however, permitted inside the tower.

Traffic
This is a popular trail for joggers, dog walkers and strollers.

Canine Swimming
Nope.

Trail Time
More than one hour.

22

Peoples
State Forest

The Park

In 1901, Connecticut became first state in the nation to appoint a state forester and to use state funds to purchase land for the establishment of state forests. In 1922, Alain White of Litchfield and Jessie Gerard of New Haven proposed that a state forest be established using donations from private individuals who paid $8 to buy one acre of land.

Barkhamsted was selected as the location for the new forest and in 1923, the first land was purchased. The next year 3,000 people gathered to witness the dedication of Peoples State Forest (the first state forest not to carry the name of a local Indian tribe) on the east bank of the Farmington River.

Today's forest covers more than 3,000 acres and is a working forest where lumber products are harvested and sold to help finance the State of Connecticut budget.

Litchfield

Phone Number
- (860) 379-0922

Website
- www.ct.gov/dep/cwp/view.asp?a=2716&q=325054

Admission Fee
- None except seasonally on the weekends and holidays

Park Hours
- Sunrise to sunset

Directions
- *Barkhamsted*; from Route 8 exit onto Route 44 East. Go north on Route 318, cross the bridge over the Farmington River and make a left on East River Road. The parking lot at the recreation area is a mile on the left and further down the road are pull-off parking for trailheads.

The Walks

When you bring your dog to Peoples State Forest, come prepared to hike. The trail system covers more than 10 miles and once you set out you won't be getting back for awhile. And you'll be getting right down to it - heading uphill from East River Road immediately. If you are in a hurry to reach the impressive views from Chougham Lookout you can take your dog straight up the rocky face of the ridge on the *Jesse Girard Trail* or you can swing around to the east.

It took alot of charcoal to fuel northwest Connecticut's world famous iron industry. This museum exhibit shows how a collier burned charcoal to obtain high grade iron.

The ridgetop views are the trail highlights but there are plenty of other curiosities, both natural and manmade in the forest. The *Agnes Bowen Trail* meanders along a swamp lubricated by beaver dams. Impressive glacial boulders dot the hillsides. You will pass foundation ruins of houses, an old cheese box factory, a soapstone quarry and the remains of a stagecoach settlement known as the Barkhamsted Lighthouse.

Trail Sense: The trailheads are clearly marked with signs and the trails are well-blazed. Use the map to plan your route ahead of time - you may need to use roads to close loops.

Dog Friendliness
Dogs are allowed throughout the forest.
Traffic
Bicycles on roads only; the hilly terrain keeps casual strollers to a minimum.
Canine Swimming
Your dog can easily score a swim in the Farmington River but nothing more than an occasional splash on the trails.
Trail Time
Several hours.

23

Kettletown
State Park

The Park

The Pootatucks were a prosperous branch of the Algonquin Indians who hunted and farmed here for hundreds of years. Legend has it that early British settlers traded a brass kettle for the rights to hunt and fish along the Housatonic River.

The State of Connecticut purchased land for the park in 1950 with funds left by Edward Carrington of New Haven, which he had dedicated to the acquisition of public land in the Naugatuck Valley.

The Walks

If you are looking for the prototypical Connecticut woodland, this could be it - giant hemlocks giving way to mixed hardwoods, rocky outcrops, stone walls, short climbs through hilly terrain. There are two ways for your dog to gather this quintessential Connecticut experience at Kettletown State Park.

New Haven

Phone Number
- (203) 264-5678

Website
- www.ct.gov/dep/cwp/view.asp?a=2716&q=325230

Admission Fee
- None except seasonally on the weekends and holidays

Park Hours
- 8:00 a.m. to sunset

Directions
- *Southbury*; take Exit 15 off I-84. Go south on Route 67 and make a right at the first light onto Kettletown Road. After three miles turn right on Georges Hill Road to the park in a half-mile on the left.

Casual canine hikers will want to head up the *William Miller Trail* on rock-studded old fire roads. The destination is a pair of overlooks of the greenish-brown Lake Zoar below. The rocky perches are shrouded by trees that camoflauge sharp drop-offs, especially from the northen ledge, so take care with your dog. After the overlooks, the 1.75-mile loop levels out as it rounds the knob but you can shorten the hike by cutting over the hillock.

Hardy canine hikers will want to tackle the *Pomeraug/Crest Trail* that delivers similar lake vistas and more rigorous hill-climbing in a 3.5-mile loop.

The two ridge running trails are linked by thepicturesque *Brook and Boulder Nature Trail* along the busy Kettletown Brook.

Trail Sense: The trails are not energetically marked but can be followed; a map is almost mandatory, however. Especially to locate the trailheads.

These overlooks at Kettletown seem like a part of the hillside but, in fact, mask steep drop-offs for your dog.

Dog Friendliness

Dogs are allowed to hike the trails but can not use the beach or stay in the campground.

Traffic

Recreation on Lake Zoar and picnicking around the beach are the most popular activities in Kettletown State Park. You won't find much competition for these trails.

Canine Swimming

When the summer crowds leave and the beach is closed there is easy swimming for your dog in Lake Zoar after your hike. Water is not a feature of the trails, however.

Trail Time

About one hour to complete the *William Miller Trail*; several hours on the trails south of the recreation area.

24
Bigelow Hollow State Park

The Park

The Nipmuck State Forest is Connecticut's second oldest state forest with the first parcel being acquired in 1905. Acquisitions have come steadily through the years until the total acreage has reached 9,000 acres. Bigelow Hollow State Park was created for more accessible public recreation inside the forest in 1949.

The prime attractions at Bigelow Hollow are a trio of lakes, the largest being Mashapaug Pond, from the Nipmuck Indian word for "Great Pond." The natural pond wasn't half as great as it became - in the 1880s two warring neighbors attempted to tap the water in the lake, one on the north side and one on the southside. Eventually they resolved their differences and teamed up to create the present-day 300-acre lake.

Windham

Phone Number
- (860) 684-3430

Website
- www.ct.gov/dep/cwp/view.asp?a=2716&q=325174&depNav_GID=1650.

Admission Fee
- None except seasonally on the weekends and holidays

Park Hours
- 8:00 a.m. to sunset

Directions
- *Union*; take Route 190 North from I-84 (Exit 73 or 74) to Route 171 East to the park entrance on the left.

The Walks

You can take an hour or a day with your dog in Bigelow Hollow State Park. The extensive trail system loops around two lakes and along the shore of the third. The yellow-blazed *Bigelow Pond Loop* is a good place to start your canine hiking day and it is a curious footpath indeed. Many park trails connect picnic areas but the path here runs right through the picnic sites. If it is a busy weekend you may want to pass on this hike and steer towards more private trails. As it is the eastern shore runs through a pine and hemlock woodland that leaves the path covered in paw-friendly pine straw. By the time you reach the opposite shore your dog will be picking her way along a narrow route through big rocks and big trees.

Serious canine hiking begins when you start down the Park Road, headed for the *Nipmuck Trail* around Breakneck Pond. You'll be on the trail for almost seven miles with your dog. Often times it will be rocky, other times it will be mucky. You'll even pass through some areas of nutrient-poor bogs that are home to insectivorious pitcher plants and sticky sundews.

Somewhere in between the two pond circumnavigations in the way of a challenge for your dog is the *Mashapaug Pond View Trail*. This loops offers a nice mix of elevation changes in its four-mile exploration. If you sense your dog is flagging you can use a forest road to cut this hike in half. The pretty pond is natural but the water level is increased by two dams. State record largemouth bass (12 lb, 14 oz) and brown trout (16 lb, 4 oz) have been pulled from these waters.

Trail Sense: There is a map posted on the information board if you haven't printed one off the website and it will come in handy. The main trails are blazed and key junctions feature signposts. The trails around Breakneck Pond will demand your most undivided attention here.

Dog Friendliness
Dogs are allowed throughout the state park and forest.
Traffic
The further you hike from the parking lot the more solitude you will find. The trails in the Nipmuck Forest may reveal a mountain biker or skier in the winter but there won't be many.
Canine Swimming
Some of the best access to the ponds is at the boat launch but your water-loving dog will undoubtedly find a place for a swim at some point in Bigelow Hollow. At Mashapaug Pond, try the picnic area as well.
Trail Time
A full afternoon possible.

25
Osbornedale State Park

The Park

After the Revolutionary War the parkland off Silver Hill Road was mined for silver. The venture did not last long and the metal that was to bring

New Haven

Phone Number
- (203) 735-4311

Website
- www.ct.gov/dep/cwp/view.asp?A=2716&Q=325246

Admission Fee
- None

Park Hours
- 8:00 a.m. to sunset

Directions
- *Derby*; for the trails at the Kellogg Environmental Center take Route 34 from Route 8 or the Merritt Parkway into downtown Derby. Continue west for 1.5 miles and turn right at Lakeview Terrace. At the end of the street turn left on Hawthorne Avenue and the parking lot on the left.

fortune to the region would be brass.

John White Osborne co-founded the pioneering Osborne & Cheesman Manufacturing Company and under his son Wilbur Fisk Osborne, a four-year Civil War veteran, the firm came to dominate the brass eyelet business in the United States and Europe.

Of Wilbur Osborne's four children, only the youngest, Frances Eliza, survived childhood. When she was 31 her father died. Even though she had never completed high school due to an accident that had cost her one eye and against the advice of all around her, Frances joined the very thin ranks of woman business leaders in 1907.

She skillfully expanded the family business portfolio and landholdings over the next half-century and when she died she willed 350 acres to the people of Connecticut for the state park.

The Walks

Most of the folks who come to Osbornedale State Park do so to enjoy the fishing pond or to picnic or to play on the ballfields. But canine hikers will want to literally go to the other side of the mountain. At the Kellogg estate on the Housatonic River your dog will luxuriate in the soft grass paths of the *Kestral Trail* through a high grass meadow and around the pondscape of the former pastures.

These trails are short and on a blue-sky day your dog won't be in a hurry to lose the sun on his back but for serious trail time you will need to head for the wooded hillsides. The *Red Trail* loops for 2.5 miles up and around the mountain, working across brooks and around glacial boulders. The varied landscape will keep your dog's tail wagging, even on the various steep segments.

Trail Sense: Your biggest challenge will be finding the trailheads but once you land on the trail things improve.

Dog Friendliness
Dogs are allowed to hike across Osborndale.

Traffic
Expect little competition for these trails; mountain bikes are allowed and it is suitable for skiers in the winter.

Canine Swimming
The reedy ponds at the Kellog Estate are better suited for ducks but Pickett's Pond is a great spot for your dog to swim.

Trail Time
More than one hour.

26
Cockaponset State Forest

The Park

The settlement of Haddam was made in 1662 by twenty-eight young men who settled on the east shore of the Connecticut River. When the local Indians sold the land to the English, they reserved some forty acres at Pattaquoenk. The little settlement in the center of the town called Ponset, by the settlers, was called Cockaponset by the Indians.

During the Great Depression of the 1930s, Franklin Roosevelt's Civilian Conservation Corps set up three camps in the forest - Roosevelt, Hadley and Filley - to develop recreation facilities and build roads. Today Cockaponset is Connecticut's second largest forest with over 16,000 acres.

Middlesex

Phone Number
- (860) 663-2030

Website
- www.ct.gov/dep/cwp/view.asp?a=2716&q=325056

Admission Fee
- None except seasonally on the weekends and holidays at Pattaconk Recreation Area

Park Hours
- Sunrise to sunset

Directions
- *Haddam*; From Route 9 take Exit 6 and go west on Route 148 for approximately 2 miles. Take a right onto Cedar Lake Road and drive 2 miles, turning left at the Pattaconk Lake sign.

The Walks

The Pattaconk Reservoir in the southern part of the forest is the centerpiece for most canine hiking outings. Here you will find the park's only two hiking-only trails, each leading along the west end of the water. The *Pattaconk Trail* (blue/red) and *Cockaponset Trail* (blue) can be combined to form afternoon-long loops. Expect some rocky patches (one of the reasons the forest is here is that this land was too rocky to be easily cultivated) but most of this is fairly easy going for your dog through an airy woodscape. You can also complete a circumnavigation of the two-pronged Pattaconk Reservoir by hooking into the trail down the east side of the water. this route doesn't hug the shoreline but the water is visible most of the way. The path is narrower and tigher as it twists its way along here.

The two foot paths should sate most dogs' hiking appetites but there are dozens of miles of more trails to explore in Cockaponset State Forest, traveling on abandoned access roads and fire roads. Make sure you have a map or compass, and plenty of time, because many of these routes are unmarked.

Trail Sense: The main trails are reliably blazed but you'll encounter many that aren't marked. Trail junctions will especially set your dog to sniffing and you to scratching your head.

Dog Friendliness

Dogs are allowed across the forest trails.

Traffic

Plenty of bikes and some horses but you should have no problem disappearing for long stretches with your dog if that is your wont.

Canine Swimming

The best swimming for your dog is at either end of Pattaconk Reservoir but it is not impossible to slip into the water elsewhere.

Trail Time

Many hours possible.

27
Gay City
State Park

The Park

In 1796 Elijah Andrus led a small band of devout followers out of Hartford to a secluded gorge on the Black-ledge River. The community, known as Factory Hollow, scratched out a living from the rocky soil but founder Andrus departed four years later for unkown reasons. John Gay was officially appointed secular leader of the colony and Reverend Henry P. Sumner took Andrus' place as spiritual leader.

A woolen mill was built to rescue the fortunes of the flagging band and they indeed prospered until the British blockade during the War of 1812 dried up their markets. After the war the mill revived but burned in 1830. A new rag paper operation kept economic life flickering until the Civil War drained the town of its young men. The mill burned after the war and Factory Hollow was soon a ghost town.

Tolland

Phone Number
- (860) 295-9523

Website
- www.ct.gov/dep/cwp/view.asp?A=2716&Q=325202

Admission Fee
- None except seasonally on the weekends and holidays

Park Hours
- 8:00 a.m. to sunset

Directions
- *Hebron*; on Route 85, 6.7 miles north of Route 66.

In 1953, the area was turned over to the State of Connecticut for use as a state park. In an odd conclusion to the saga of Factory Hollow, the descendants of the Sumner family, who tussled with the Gay family for control of the village in its heyday, decreed that the Gay name be used for the recreation area.

The Walks

Gay City is a good choice for a long, relaxed ramble with your dog. Much of your way will be on wide, old cart roads that have been worn down enough to be paw-friendly. You can cobble together a loop around the perimeter of the park that covers as much as five miles. When the going isn't flat, the inclines are gentle. Most of the way will be wooded but you pop out into the open air every now and then.

The 1500-acre park is laced with shortish trail segments, however, so you can come here every day for a week and never repeat your canine hiking day. The most attractive stretch may be the *White Trail* that wanders past the swimming pond and visits the stone ruins of the old mill site. Rather than being overgrown with vines only a few majestic pine trees grace the area.

The old mill ruins from Gay City don't look like they were abandoned 125 years ago.

Trail Sense: The many trails are color coded and well-blazed. If you have any doubts many trail junctions have "You are here" maps.

Dog Friendliness
Dogs are allowed on the hking trails and in the picnic areas, but not on the swimming beach.

Traffic
This is a popular park and the trails are suitable for joggers and mountain bikers.

Canine Swimming
There are three main ponds in the park; only the central swimming pond is free of vegetation. Just down the shore from the swimming area, near the water outlet, is an easy place for your dog to get in a few dog paddles.

Trail Time
More than one hour.

28

Mashamoquet Brook State Park

The Park

Today's park is part of land purchased from the local Indians in 1686. The price was 30 pounds and was known at that time as "The Mashmuket Purchase." Mashamoquet, meaning "stream of good fishing," was the largest stream flowing through the property.

Mashamoquet Brook was a source of power for small mills, some of whose ruins still exist along the pleasing stream. The restored Brayton Grist Mill stands at the park entrance and is open to visitors.

Much of the parkland was purchased by the Daughters of the American Revolution and kept as open space. The State of Connecticut bought their stake in 1924 and began adding other parcels. The present park is a melding of three previous parks and spreads over 900 acres.

Windham

Phone Number
- (860) 928-6121

Website
- www.ct.gov/dep/cwp/view.asp?a=2716&q=325238

Admission Fee
- None except seasonally on the weekends and holidays

Park Hours
- 8:00 a.m to sunset

Directions
- *Pomfret*; from I-395 take Exit 93 onto Route 101 West. Cross Route 69 to the end where the road becomes Route 44. The park is on the left. Parking for the hiking trails is on Wolf Den Drive (unpaved). Access is from Wolf Den Road off Route 44, west of the park entrance and from Route 101, just east of its end at Route 44.

The Walks

The trail system in Mashamoquet Brook is bisected by dirt-and-gravel Wolf Den Drive that makes it easy to craft hiking loops between one and two miles long. Most of the park's attractions are on the south side of the road where the terrain becomes hillier and rockier. As you make your way to such rock formations as Wolf's Den, Table Rock and Indian Chair the rock-studded dirt paths sometimes lead over bare rock where your dog will be better suited than you.

It is not all hard rock and packed dirt on these narrow, woody paths for your dog. You will also cross swampy areas as you disappear deeper into these out-of-the-way woodlands.

Trail Sense: There are no extraneous trails in the park and the trails are well-marked. Look for blazes on rocks as well as trees. Directions painted on the rocks point the way to the featured rock formations.

At the entrance to the Wolf's Den.

Dog Friendliness

Dogs are not allowed in the campground, the beach or picnic shelter but are welcome to trot the trails.

Traffic

Light foot traffic on these rough trails.

Canine Swimming

The Mashamoquet Brook is not a stop along the hiking trails but the setting for the picnic areas so a special trip is required for a doggie dip.

Trail Time

More than one hour.

29
Sessions Woods
Wildlife Management Area

The Park

Using land purchased from the United Methodist Church in 1981 the Department of Environmental Protection developed Sessions Woods as an educational wildlife habitat. The 455 acres are managed through demonstration sites, displays, group tours and self-guided hiking trails.

The Walks

The canine hiking in this quiet refuge takes places on a three-mile loop that leads to viewing blinds along marshland before ambling back. The main track is along a wide, gravel-and-dirt road that is mostly agreeable to the paw. There is one downhill and one uphill to the back of the property in this easy, shady exploration of Sessions Woods.

Hartford

Phone Number
- (860) 675-8130

Website
- www.ct.gov/dep/cwp/view.
asp?a=2723&q=326220&depN
av_GID=1655

Admission Fee
- None

Park Hours
- Sunrise to sunset

Directions
- *Burlington*; east of Route 8.
From Route 6 take Route 69
north for three miles to the
entrance on the left.

The loop is closed on the *Tree ID Trail* that slips through the moist East Negro Hill Brook valley. The footpath has its rooty and rocky spots before mellowing out. Short sidetrips lead down wooden steps to a seasonal waterfall and up the metal steps of a lookout tower that peeks over the treetops.

The *Deer Sign Trail* is a short loop that introduces wildlife management techniques for small parcels of land, including backyards. Check out the bat shelter that aids insect control and plantings of shrubs that benefit wildlife.

Trail Sense: A map is available and there are plenty of signs out on the trail to keep you rolling in the right direction.

The flow in the waterfall on Negro Hill Brook is controlled by beaver activity upstream - and sometimes it just trickles down.

Dog Friendliness

Dogs are allowed on these trails but if you are the type who likes to let go of the leash every now and then take your dog someplace else - signs every few yards admonish you of the evils dogs can do to nesting birds.

Traffic

No horses, hunters or motorized vehicles; you may have to maneuver your dog past a school group at times.

Canine Swimming

A splash here or there is all.

Trail Time

About one hour.

30
Rock Spring Preserve

The Park

The town of Scotland was formed in 1700 by, naturally, a Scottish emigrant named Isaac Magoon. Ten years later George Lilly purchased land on both sides of Little River, a tributary of the Shetucket River. The early settlers farmed some good land in the Little River valley where they could find it and the town has remained much the same for three centuries.

This land was purchased by David Shoemaker in 1938. Born into an affluent Pittsburgh, Pennsylvania family, Shoemaker had decided to abandon his career as an artist and move to Connecticut with his wife to become a gentleman farmer. He began to buy parcels of land, raise pygmy goats and rare breeds of cattle and to experiment with various crops and farming techniques.

Windham

Phone Number
- None

Website
- www.nature.org/wherewe-work/northamerica/states/con-necticut/preserves/art5368.html

Admission Fee
- None

Park Hours
- Sunrise to sunset

Directions
- *Scotland*; take Exit 83 off I-395 onto Route 97. Head north and turn right on Route 14 (Palmer Road) for 0.5 mile, then take a left back onto Route 97 for 1.4 miles. The Preserve and parking area are on the right.

An early land preservationist, as well as a charter member of the Scotland Volunteer Fire Department, Shoemaker actively worked to encourage the community to appreciate the natural value of their land. In 1974 he donated 436 acres to The Nature Conservancy for the creation of a wildlife refuge that was to become Rock Spring Preserve.

The Walks

Every pawfall of your dog's journey in the quiet Rock Spring Preserve will be under the leafy canopy of a mixed hardwood and pine forest. The main trail utilizes an old wagon road. Your dog will find some rocky patches but most of the way will be paw-friendly. There are plenty of ups and downs and a glacially-formed landscape that delivers something new over each ridge.

The white-blazed *Perimeter Trail* works downhill to a stretch along the secluded Little River. It can be tough going along the stream where the footpath narrows and the understory gets hearty in the summer. After circling the 445-acre preserve you will have covered a bit more than three miles.

The namesake spring of the preserve is capped but cool water still flows into a small brook.

Trail Sense: A faded map posted on the information board is your only orientation to the side trails in the preserve. Bring a piece of paper and pencil to sketch it before starting out.

Dog Friendliness
Dogs are typically banned from Nature Conservancy properties but there are no posted prohibitions here - perhaps in deference to David Shoemaker, an animal lover who kept a pet skunk in his menagerie.

Traffic
The parking lot is only big enough for a handful of cars.

Canine Swimming
The slow-moving Little River is wide enough for a lazy swim.

Trail Time
More than one hour.

3I
Tunxis
State Forest

The Park

Tunxis State Forest covers over 9,000 acres on both sides of the Barkhamsted Reservoir. When the first lands were acquired in 1923 they were already heavily forested, unlike most of Connecticut's other forests that were recovering from centuries of cutting and harvesting.

Today, Tunxis remains undeveloped, actively managed for improved forest health and diversity, and to produce forest products.

The Walks

The attraction for canine hikers in the wilds of the Tunxis Forest is a massive jumble of boulders known as the Indian Council Caves, but to quote Harry Chapin, "it's got to be the going, not the getting there that's good." And to going to the caves is quite good indeed.

The trip along the *Tunxis Trail* covers a tick over two miles. Your dog will find enough moderate climbs to hold her interest but plenty of easy stretches as well. You'll pass through a mature pine grove, hillsides blanketed in cinnamon and Christmas ferns and finish with some scrambling across boulders. These boulder crossings are the easiest and safest for your dog in western Connecticut.

When you reach the caves there is a tricky vertical descent but if your dog can't negotiate it, you can bypass this drop by using a faint trail through the mountain laurel to the right. This side route is especially handy when heading back.

Trail Sense: There aren't as many blazes as you might ideally want for this narrow, twisting trail but you can still hike confidently without a map; more importantly, it is well-marked at road crossings.

The Indian Council Caves are your dog's ultimate destination on this pass of the Tunxis Trail.

Dog Friendliness

Dogs are allowed to hike the *Tunxis Trail*.

Traffic

Maybe you will see another trail user on a weekend. Maybe.

Canine Swimming

Seasonal streams may provide a refresher along the trail but no swimming.

Trail Time

About two hours to complete the four-mile round trip out and back.

"Dogs' lives are too short. Their only fault, really."
-Agnes Sligh Turnbull

32

Gillette Castle
State Park

The Park

In 1913, when he was 60 years old and world famous as the stage portrayor of Sherlock Holmes, William Gillette sailed down the Connecticut River and past a chain of hills known as the Seven Sisters. He docked at the southernmost hill, clambered up to a viewpoint and knew he had found his retirement spot.

The actor and playright designed the castle and its interior himself and over the next six years a team of laborers crafted Gillette's 24-room vision of native fieldstone in the style of a Norman fortress. Gillette, son of a former United States Senator and direct descendant of Thomas Hooker, the founder of Hartford, would tinker with his masterpiece until his death in 1937. Childless and a widower for half-a-century, Gillette's will protected the property against any "blithering saphead" who might destroy his creation and the State of Connecticut became its steward in 1943.

Middlesex

Phone Number
- (860) 526-2336

Website
- www.ct.gov/dep/cwp/view. asp?A=2716&Q=325204

Admission Fee
- None for the grounds

Park Hours
- 8:00 a.m. to sunset

Directions
- *East Haddam*; The park is off Route 82. Use Exit 22 from I-91 or Exit 69 for I-95.

The Walks

The pride and joy of William Gillette's 184-acre estate was his three-mile narrow gauge railroad that looped through the woods below the castle. Gillette decorated the route with fanciful bridges, a wooden trestle and an arched tunnel blasted through bedrock. The rails are gone but the bed makes a unique pathway for your dog's travels through the park. The terrain is hilly enough that your dog might wish he could hop a ride on that train but most of the grades work around the hillsides rather than using harsh vertical climbs.

Dogs are not allowed inside the castle walls but the trail does lead to Grand Central Station where you will be able to see Gillette's unique home.

Trail Sense: None of the trails or trailheads are marked but you will be able to pick up the trails easily from the lower parking lot and entrance road.

Dog Friendliness

Dogs are not allowed inside the castle walls but are welcome to explore the park grounds and use the picnic area.

Traffic

This is one of the crown jewels of the Connecticut state park system but most of the visitors are here to tour the castle.

Canine Swimming

There are places for your dog to slip into the ornamental ponds on a hot day but not for extensive canine aquatics.

Trail Time

About one hour.

One of the elaborate stone-and-wood bridges that grace the trails in Gillette State Park.

33

West Rock Ridge State Park

The Park

West Rock Ridge is a volcanic traprock formation that rises up to 627 feet above sea leavel as it runs roughly north by northwest from the town of New Haven. The West Rock Ridge State Park and its Advisory Council were established in 1975 as the result of a local grass roots movement to protect the land from development and communication towers. West Rock Ridge is the only State Park in Connecticut to have its own Advisory Council. The council is made up of 3 members from each of the adjoining towns (Bethany, Woodbridge, Hamden and New Haven), and 3 appointees from the State Department of Environmental Protection.

The Walks

West Rock Ridge runs for about six miles and is laced with multi-use trails frequented by mountain bikers and hardy canine hikers. Like the rock itself these paths can be rough and stony under paw. Connecting trails between the parallel upper ridge and lower ridge trails will provide most of your dog's workout in the park.

For canine hikers looking for something a bit less rugged there is a 1.5-mile loop around Lake Wintergreen. This serene ramble uses old roads through mixed conifer and hardwood forests to circumnavigate the shallow waters.

Trail Sense: Don't try the ridge without a map from the website. Even with a map the trails can be unreliably marked.

New Haven

Phone Number
- (203) 789-7498

Website
- ct.gov/dep/cwp/view.asp?A=2716&Q=325276

Admission Fee
- None

Park Hours
- 8:00 a.m. to sunset

Directions
- *Hamden*; From the Merritt Parkway (Route 15), take Exit 60 and turn right onto Dixwell Avenue/Route 10 South. Turn right onto Benham and follow to the end, making a left on Main Street. Lake Wintergreen will be on your right and the main entrance will be further along after taking a right on Wintergreen Avenue and passing under the Parkway (on the right).

Edward Whalley and his son-in-law William Goffe were close supporters of Oliver Cromwell and trusted commanders in his army during the English Civil War. Upon the defeat of King Charles I, Whalley was one who signed the death warrant for the King in 1649. Cromwell's Protectorate was short-lived as he died from malaria in 1658. During the Restoration under Charles II, Whalley and Goffe fled to Massachusetts. Warrants for their arrest shortly followed and the pair fled to New Haven where they could count on a sympathetic populace, including another judge, John Dixwell, who, like Whalley, had tried King Charles. Whalley and Goffe hid in cellars but were soon flushed out by Royalist troops. They fled to the safety of a cave in the rock formations of West Rock Ridge where they lived for months, eluding their pursuers who were unfamiliar with the landscape. The regicides never were apprehended but lived out their ruined lives in secret. None too pleased with the actions of the New Haven townsfolk, King Charles II suppressed their petition to govern as a separate colony and attached them instead to Connecticut.

Dog Friendliness

Dogs are allowed to enjoy the trails throughout the park.

Traffic

The blue-blazed trail is for hikers-only, as are some other paths but most of the park is open to bikes. Some of the most disagreeable traffic, however, won't clog the trails - the hum from nearby Merritt Parkway is overwhelming in spots.

Canine Swimming

Lake Wintergreen is a super swimming hole for water-loving dogs with some easy access points.

Trail Time

Less than an hour around Lake Wintergreen to a full day on the ridge.

34
Southford Falls State Park

The Park

The importance of the falls on Eight Mile Brook have mirrored the rise and fall of American industry. Until 1843 only a small sawmill and grist mill operated here. In 1855, as the Industrial Revolution intensified, a bustling paper mill producing straw paper boards was built here.

As America elbowed to the forefront of world business in the 1890s, the Diamond Match Company purchased the Southford Mill to churn out matchbooks, The match conglomerate had just purchased the new patent for matchbooks from Joshua Pusey for $4,000 and needed more capacity.

In 1924, the entire paper mill portion of the plant was destroyed by fire and Southford Falls began to revert to nature. Today, with most former American factories shuttered, the falls provide only a few skeletal stone remains as testament to its proud industrial past as well.

New Haven

Phone Number
- (203) 264-5169

Website
- www.ct.gov/dep/cwp/view.asp?A=2716&Q=325266

Admission Fee
- None

Park Hours
- Sunrise to sunset

Directions
- *Oxford*; from I-84 take Exit 16 onto Route 188. Go to the junction with Route 67 South. When Route 188 goes right at the next light follow it to the park on the left.

The Walks

The parking lot here is right at the falls and as you meander past a lazy fishing pond your dog has every reason to believe this will be a trail day of no great consequence. The impression doesn't change as you mosey down an old woods road along the tumbling cascades and chutes of the Eight Mile Brook and cross a boardwalk through the bottomlands.

And then the *Larkin Bridle Trail* muscles up. The gravelly road fades away and your dog will soon be picking her way on soft dirt and rocks up a hemlock-sprinkled slope. The climbs are short enough that any dog can handle this hike but demanding enough to set tongues to panting.

At the top of the ridge a little spur leads further uphill to a two-story metal tower anchored to a rock. Only an agility dog will be able to conquer the open wooden steps but the tower isn't high enough to see over the treetops so you may want to skip the sidetrip altogether. The rest of this frisky two-mile canine hike rolls back down the hillside to Papermill Pond where your dog can cool off and roll around in a grassy area.

Trail Sense: The route is blazed well enough to follow without a map and the bridge and tower are signed.

Dog Friendliness
Dogs are welcome in the picnic areas and on the hiking trails.

Traffic
This is a lightly used park, especially if you come during the week or hike with your dog past the end of the falls and boardwalk.

Canine Swimming
Your dog can splash in the plunge pools or swim in Papermill Pond if he finds a non-marshy spot.

Trail Time
About one hour.

Southford Falls spills down from Papermill Pond in multiple cascades and chutes.

35
Babcock
Preserve

The Park

The largest park in Greenwich was once a patchwork of cropland and orchards, neatly defined by miles of stone walls. In 1880 the Greenwich Water Company bought the land to protect the watershed of Putnam Reservoir. They left the land to regenerate, protecting the purity of the water.

In 1937 the building of the Merritt Parkway left the resevoir stranded on the wrong side of Greenwich and 304 acres were sold to Charles Henry Babcock and Mary Reynolds Babcock, an heir to the R.J. Reynolds Tobacco Company fortune. The Babcocks had departed Greenwich for North Carolina by this time and the property was left in its natural state and not developed residentially.

Fairfield
Phone Number - (203) 622-7814
Website - None
Admission Fee - None
Park Hours - Sunrise to sunset
Directions - *Greenwich*; from Route 15 (Merritt Parkway) take Exit 31 onto North Street. Go north, passing a reservoir on your right. The Preserve entrance through stone walls will be on the left.

In 1972 the town of Greenwich acquired the property from conservation-minded Babcock heirs and it has remained an open space for passive recreation.

The Walks

The first thing you need to know about Babcock Preserve is that there are *two* separate mapboards. The one you encounter at the parking lot is a Google Earth-type aerial shot that will leave you feeling as if you should have brought a team of St. Bernard rescue dogs. Walk down the main trail road a bit, however, and you will find a Boy Scout mapboad that deciphers the many trails in such a way that you can plan your dog's day at Babcock with confidence.

This is a woodland of mixed hardwoods made for rambling. The terrain is kind of lumpy and a bit scruffy, maybe overgrown in spots. All to the good for your dog. The hiking is gentle throughout, a little more challenging off the main *Yellow Birch* trunk trail but nothing that will keep your dog's tail from wagging. There may be more stone walls here than any woodland in Connecticut.

Fieldstone walls like this one along the Ruins Trail are a dominant theme of canine hiking around Babcock Preserve.

Trail Sense: It is easy to get turned around in Babcock Preserve so keep your eyes peeled for the next blaze. Signs at some trail junctions are welcome finds.

Dog Friendliness
Dogs are permitted at Babcock Preserve.

Traffic
This is not a busy park but you can meet the occasional horse; bikes are not allowed.

Canine Swimming
Your dog may chance upon a vernal pool or seasonal stream. One place that holds water deep enough for a brief paddle throughout the year is conveniently situated along the *Red Maple Trail* near the North Street parking lot so your dog can finish her hike with a refreshing dip.

Trail Time
More than one hour.

36
Nehantic
State Forest

The Park

This land was once the territory of Uncas, an Indian chief born in the Pequot territory. He rebelled against the tribe and was expelled, traveling eastward and forming with his followers the Mohegan tribe, taking an ancient title the Pequots once held. Through numerous skirmishes with warring tribes Uncas expanded his territiory throughout the 17th century. In every dust-up Uncas was a staunch ally of the English colonists, so much so that in 1825 a granite obelisk was erected in his honor in Norwich with General Andrew Jackson laying the cornerstone.

The Nehantic Forest was the first state forest in New London County, with the first land purchased in 1925. Like much of the surrounding land, the

New London

Phone Number
- (860) 526-2336

Website
- www.ct.gov/dep/cwp/view.asp?A=2716&Q=325064

Admission Fee
- None

Park Hours
- 8:00 a.m. to sunset

Directions
- *Lyme*; From Exit 70 off I-95 follow Route 156 north to park entrance at Uncas Pond. This is a washboard dirt road. An alternate entrance can be found to the north on Beaver Brook Road east to Keeny Road.

forest had a long history of farming and much of tree cover today is a second growth of hardwoods.

The Walks

This is meat-and-potatoes hiking with your dog - no great destinations but a solid day with your dog in undeveloped forest land. The route of choice is over the blue-blazed *Nayantaquit Trail* that is a stacked-loop affair with legs to trailheads at Uncas Lake and Keeney Road.

You will be crossing stone reminders of an inhabited past, slipping through boulder foundations and traversing several ridges en route to Nickerson Hill, the high point of the forest at 452 feet. Some of the ascents will set your dog to panting but nothing that will dampen her enthusiasm. The big loop covers a bit over four miles.

Trail Sense: The forest is pockmarked with fire roads, some of which you will want to use but most that you don't so keep an eye on the blazes.

Dog Friendliness

Dogs are allowed throughout the forest.

Traffic

Expect long periods of solitude on the trail with your dog.

Canine Swimming

The streams on the trail may offer splashing but little more; starting at Uncas Pond adds length to your canine hike but gives your dog a chance to finish the day with a refreshing swim.

Trail Time

Two to three hours on the *Nayantaquit Trail*.

37
Black Rock
State Park

The Park

Black Rock gots its name from graphite lead that attracted early miners. Stone arrowheads and primitive tools have been found in the area as well. As you climb these footpaths you will still see specks of mica sparkling in the rocks.

Black Rock Forest, a citizen's conservation group gave this slice of the Western Highlands to the people of Connecticut in 1926.

The Walks

This is destination-oriented hiking for your dog along the blue-blazed *Mattatuck Trail*. To the north is the namesake Black Rock and its view of

Litchfield
Phone Number - (860) 567-5694
Website - www.ct.gov/dep/cwp/view. asp?a=2716&q=325176
Admission Fee - A daily parking fee in season
Park Hours - 8:00 a.m. to sunset
Directions - *Watertown*; from Route 8, take Exit 38 onto Route 6 West. The park entrance is on the right.

the valley, reached with a stiff, rocky climb. Black Rock is less than a mile away though; you can extend the trip a bit further north to loop back on the red-blazed trail or retrace your steps.

To the south is Leatherman Cave, a bit over a mile away. This canine hike starts with an uphill climb and when you head back from the cave you have to start with another uphill climb. In between are bare-rock ledges that are unfenced where your dog will have to scramble above steep drop-offs. Except for one spot there is plenty of room to traverse the ledges safely with your dog but don't let your guard down. At the top of the cave you can spread out with your dog on Crane Lookout and enjoy some views above the trees.

Trail Sense: The trail is blazed; not much else to help you except a sign at Leatherman Cave - stay on the *Mattatuck Trail* here, not the *Jericho Trail*.

Bonus
This is not *the* Leatherman Cave but rather *a* Leatherman Cave, one of many between the Connecticut and Hudson rivers. The Leatherman first appeared sometime around the Civil War, when it was not unusual to find intransient men roaming the countryside looking for work, a meal or a barn in which to spend the night. The Leatherman stood out from his brethren for several reasons. He never spoke, favoring a mumbling form of communication, and he was dressed head-to-toe in a hand-made leather outfit. He would make a circuit through Connecticut and New York arriving at the same villages and farmhouses on a ritual that he kept to for a quarter-century.

He often spent the night in rock shelters like this one, neatly arranging a bed of pine needles and stacking firewood for his return. Of course rumors swirled as to his true identity. The most popular was that he was a Frenchman named Jules Bourglay whose life was ruined when he accidentally burned down his fiancee's father's leather factory. When he was found dead in the winter of 1889 a French prayer book was found among his possessions but nothing more to solve his mystery.

The Leatherman is buried in Sparta Cemetery in Ossining, New York. The headstone, identifying him as "Jules Bourglay of Lyons, France", was placed on his grave by local historians in 1953.

Dog Friendliness

Dogs are allowed to hike the trails but are not permitted on the beach or in the campground.

Traffic

Only serious canine hikers need apply so don't expect a parade in these woods.

Canine Swimming

You can get your dog in Black Rock Pond but it is not on the main hiking trails.

Trail Time

Several hours.

38
Day Pond
State Park

The Park

The Day family built the small pond to power its sawmill back in the days when so many mills lined the Salmon River that they couldn't all operate at the same time. When the water supply in the river became insufficient some mills operated at night and others during the day.

Today the Salmon River, the largest stream contained wholly in Connecticut, is packed mostly by fishermen. The State Board of Fisheries and Game began buying land here in 1934 and Day Pond State Park and the surrounding Salmon River State Forest comprise more than 6,000 acres.

New London

Phone Number
- (860) 295-9523

Website
- www.ct.gov/dep/cwp/view.asp?a=2716&q=325218

Admission Fee
- None except seasonally on the weekends and holidays

Park Hours
- 8:00 a.m. to sunset

Directions
- *Colchester*; take Exit 16 off Route 2. Follow Route 149S for 3 miles and then take a hard right onto Peck Lane. Turn left onto Day Pond Road to park.

The Walks

The marquee walk here is the *Salmon River Trail* that loops around the Day Pond Brook. Once you set out with your dog you are signing on for at least a three-mile hike but most first-time visitors will want to tack on the two-mile *Comstock Bridge Connector* that leads to the historic 19th-century covered bridge. Completing this out-and-back trail segment will push your total canine hike to almost seven miles.

The terrain is moderate and shaded throughout as the narrow path twists through glacial erratics and mixed forest. On the trail to the Comstock Bridge it gets a bit hillier but any moderately athletic dog will love this hike. Around Day Pond you will find a *Nature Trail* suitable mostly as a leg-stretcher as you pick your way among rocks and a rich understory.

Trail Sense: You can navigate the *Salmon River Trail* without a map if one is not available - just follow the blue blazes.

Dog Friendliness

Dogs are permitted on the trails and in the picnic areas but not on the Day Pond beach.

Traffic

Most park users come to picnic or swim and not take a three-hour hike so expect long stretches of solitude on the trail with your dog.

Canine Swimming

In the off-season the open water and sandy beach of Day Pond are a swimming dog's paradise. Out on the trail the route crosses tributaries of the Salmon River and if you reach Comstock Bridge your dog can celebrate with a refreshing dip.

Trail Time

Several hours.

39
Bluff Head Preserve

The Park

Bluff Head is a ridge of molten rock that pushed through a fault in the earth's surface 200 million years ago. The fault line that led to the formation of Bluff Head runs under Route 77 and the gap was clearly visible before the construction of the roadway. At this point the geology of Connecticut changes dramatically, to the east are the remains of an ancient seabed and to the west is found mostly dark brown baslatic traprock.

The Guilford Land Conservation Trust began buying land at Bluff Head in the 1960s. Today, it owns more than 500 acres there, including most of the area around the sheer, 500-foot trap-rock cliff as well as the adjoining areas of Totoket Mountain.

Middlesex

Phone Number
- None

Website
- www.guilfordlandtrust.org/bluffhead.html

Admission Fee
- None

Park Hours
- Sunrise to sunset

Directions
- *Durham*; the trailhead is on the west side of Route 77, 4.2 miles south of the junction with Route 17.

The Walks

You have your choice of how to attack the Bluff Head ridge. If your dog prefers a more gradual ascent and doesn't mind a straight-down, all-out descent, take the *Bluff Loop Trail* that leaves on the Fire Tower Road to the left. If your dog favors a safer climb down and a heartier hike up, take the blue-blazed *Mattabesett Trail* up the scree-covered slope to your right.

If you don't have a lot of time to spend at Bluff Head you can walk along the ridge and re-trace your steps to complete your loop. Hiking is easy atop Bluff Head with trees growing to the edge. Where it does open for overlooks, keep you dog back from the precipitous edges and soak in the long views to the east, north to Hartford and south to Long Island Sound. The loop trail back into Totoket Mountain is a pleasant ramble through formerly logged-out woods.

Look for a double-trunked oak directly on the trail that holds a pocket for rainwater that serves as a convenient drinking bowl for your dog.

You can also plan a full canine hiking day at Bluff Head. Tie the *Lone Pine Trail* (it comes by its name honestly) that runs across Route 77 through the valley to Braemore Preserve onto the *Mattabesett Trail* through the Rockland Preserve and the Broomstick Ledges. The climbs will be more gradual over here so your athletic dog should have the energy to complete this ten-mile loop.

Trail Sense: You can consult a detailed mapboard at Schoolhouse Brook; just follow the blue blazes and ignore the unmarked dirt bands that lead away from it in the other preserves.

Dog Friendliness
Dogs are allowed to enjoy these trails.

Traffic
No hunting and no motorized vehicles are permitted on the trails and you should find long stretches of solitude with your dog, especially on the east side of Route 77.

Canine Swimming
Swimming is not a highlighted feature of canine hiking at Bluff Head; expect a seasonal brook or two.

Trail Time
About one hour to complete the loop to Bluff Head and back, several hours more are possible along the *Mattabesett Trail*.

"They are superior to human beings as companions. They do not quarrel or argue with you. They never talk about themselves but listen to you while you talk about yourself, and keep an appearance of being interested in the conversation."
-Jerome K. Jerome

40
Hurd
State Park

The Park

John Hurd emigrated with his family from the Scottish Highlands to Massachusetts around 1685. His son Jacob came to Middle Haddam on the Connecticut River in the early 1700s. The family became involved in shipbuilding and during the American Revolution three Hurd brothers were imprisoned at the same time on a British prison ship in New York harbor.

Through marriage the Hurd family became entwined with the powerful Dart family and Russel Dart donated the land for the present day park. Hurd State Park started in 1914, one year after the establishment of the State Park Commission.

Middlesex

Phone Number
- (860) 526-2336

Website
- ct.gov/dep/cwp/view.asp?A=2716&Q=325224

Admission Fee
- None

Park Hours
- 8:00 a.m. to sunset

Directions
- *East Hampton*; on the east bank of the Connecticut River. The entrance is on Route 151, three miles south of Cobalt center on Route 66.

The Walks

The two main attractions here are each reached by short trail but don't let your dog get lulled into thinking it will just be a lazy walk in the park. The hike to the Connecticut River shore is only a half-mile loop but the climb back from the swim in the river will get your dog to panting. The easier direction to tackle the *River Trail* is counter-clockwise down the park road and back up the switchbacking foot trail.

In the opposite direction from river level is the landmark Split Rock, recognized for centuries by boaters on the Connecticut River as it peeks above the forest. Foot trails lead to several vantage points overlooking the river valley and across to White Mountain. Be careful with your dog around Split Rock because she can tumble into the trademark gap.

If your dog is just getting warmed up after visiting these points of interest you can parse together loops approaching three miles across these heavily wooded hillsides. No matter how long you decide to spend in Hurd State Park your dog will likely be sleeping on the ride home.

Trail Sense: The main trails and junctions are well-marked; if you do get off track you won't be for long as the park is constricted by a long entrance road and the Connecticut River.

Dog Friendliness

Dogs are allowed throughout the park but can't stay in the small campground that is reserved for boaters.

Traffic

Mountain bikes are allowed on the trails but this isn't a heavily used park.

Canine Swimming

There is easy access for your dog from pebbly beaches along the Connecticut River for deep water canine aquatics.

Trail Time

More than one hour.

41
Mohawk
State Forest

The Park

Mohawk State Forest, opened in 1921 as the sixth oldest forest in the state system, operates more as a sanctuary as dictated in its charter - it is the only Connecticut forest that does not allow hunting. Land for the forest was donated by the White Memorial Trust, benefactors of so much of the public lands in the Litchfield Hills. Today it is better know for the Mohawk Mountain Ski Area in winter than as a hiking mecca.

Mohawk Indians, incidentally, never lived here. The name is said to derive from signal fires lit on the mountain by local tribes to warn of potential Mohawk war parties.

Litchfield

Phone Number
- (860) 491-3620

Website
- www.ct.gov/dep/cwp/view.asp?A=2716&Q=325060

Admission Fee
- None

Park Hours
- Sunrise to sunset

Directions
- *Cornwall*; from Route 7 follow Route 4 east to the entrance on the right.

The Walks

Your canine hiking day around Mohawk Mountain will be spent mostly on the *Mohawk Trail* that actually was the route of the original *Appalachian Trail* through Connecticut before it was relocated to the west. Unless you tie in with park roads and fire roads this will be out-and-back hiking and there are several destinations to aim at.

There have been four lookout towers built on top of the 1600-foot plus Mohawk Mountain. The first was built of logs and the last (still standing but not open to the public) was the only one in Connecticut still operating in 1985 when the state switched to airplane fire detection. A loop with the paved Tourney Road can combine Mohawk Tower and Cunningham Tower in a two-mile trip.

On July 10, 1989, a line of mid-day thunderstorms spun off a series of tornadoes that carved a narrow path of destruction from Cornwall to New

Haven. The terrifying force of the winds was brief as it ripped through the forest but in minutes one of the grandest stands of old growth white pine and hemlock east of the Mississippi River known as the Cathedral Pines was destroyed. Of the original 40 acres, less than five remain. You can still see a handful of 150-foot pines along the trail in the western edge of *Mohawk Trail* and see evidence of the tornado damage in the forest.

A narrow boardwalk trail leads into the Black Spruce Bog, past showy cinnamon ferns like these.

This is hardy fare for your trail companion with challenging uphills but plenty of long, level stretches as well.

Trail Sense: A map is handy in identifying the unmarked fire roads that pop up here and there.

Dog Friendliness
Dogs are allowed to enjoy these trails.
Traffic
Light foot traffic most times of the year.
Canine Swimming
Don't get your dog's hopes up with promises of a swim here.
Trail Time
Many hours possible.

42

Giuffrida Park

The Park

Jonathan Gilbert was born in Yardley, county Worcester, England in 1617. He migrated to this area in his early adult years and established the first European farm in the region. It was known as the Meriden Farm, from which the town took its name. Gilbert's oldest daughter (from a second marriage) would marry Andrew Belcher, considered Boston's most opulent merchant and he would continue farming operations here.

The quartz foundations on the ridges in the area gave folks the idea that gold may be in dem there hills. As early as 1735 attempts were made to find that elusive vein of gold but none was ever found.

Connecticut Light and Power purchased this land to run high-voltage lines and sold the rest to the Town of Meriden that maintains the park as part of its open space program.

Hartford

Phone Number
- (203) 234-7555

Website
- ctparks.net/meriden/giuffrida/

Admission Fee
- None

Park Hours
- Sunrise to sunset

Directions
- *Meriden*; from I-691 take the Broad Street exit into town, heading north. After a half-mile turn right on Westfield Road. Stay on Westfield as it twists and turns to the park on the left.

The Walks

You can get a perfectly good hike with your dog in Giuffrida Park by circling the wooded shores of the reservoir. The terrain is seldom taxing and often wide and easy - stop at a waterside bench on this leisurely canine hike. But more athletic dogs will be itching to get up into the hillsides and there are plenty of trails to get you there.

The blue-blazed *Mattabessett Trail* takes you up to Chauncey Peak and its exposed rocky summit. Expect some steep sections and some rough going for your dog on loose rocks but these sections don't last long. Once on the ridge the woodsy going is much easier. The loop back down to Crescent Lake should take about two hours. But since you are alrady up there, consider taking the dog north for a picturesque ridgetop ramble on the ledges of Mount Lamentation, named after a settler got lost here for three days in 1636.

Trail Sense: If you are just looking for a spin around the lake with your dog you can set out right from the parking lot with confidence - just choose the trail that hugs the water; if you are planning a more extended exploration, get a map before you come.

Dog Friendliness

Dogs are allowed in the park and on the trails but Giuffrida Park may sport more "dogs on leash" signs per square foot than any park in Connecticut.

Traffic

Light foot traffic once you get into the trail system away from the populated areas of the park. Mountain bikers can use the trail system but are not allowed on the blue-blazed trails.

Canine Swimming

No dogs in the water.

Trail Time

More than one hour.

43
Mansfield Hollow
State Park

The Park

In 1952 the Army Corps of Engineers erected a large earthen dam here to prevent seasonal flooding on the Natchaug River. The lake that formed covers 500 acres and can hold 700 million gallons of water. The land is still owned by the Corps and the State of Connecticut leases over 2,000 acres for use as a state park and wildlife management area.

The Walks

With one of the largest lakes in southern New England, hiking is not the star in this park. But while most folks are out boating and dropping a line for largemouth bass, perch, crappie and eels, your dog can enjoy a relaxing day on Mansfield Hollow's eclectic trails.

There are alot of bumps and rumps on the dirt trails that lead to overlooks of the lake, enough to keep your dog's interest and double as a ski trail in the winter. A fun out-and-back walk is along the flood control levee that stretches more than one mile.

The main trails are wide

Windham

Phone Number
- (860) 928-6121

Website
- www.ct.gov/dep/cwp/view.
asp?A=2716&Q=325236

Admission Fee
- None

Park Hours
- 8:00 a.m. to sunset

Directions
- *Mansfield*; on Bassetts Bridge Road off Route 195. Take Exit 68 off I-84 East.

No swimming is allowed in Mansfield Hollow Lake but a small swimming hole near the boat ramp parking lot takes your dog into deep water in one easy step.

and paw-friendly for the most part and, with a short walk on the road, you can circle a chunk of the lake with your dog. The trip will cover more than four miles.

Trail Sense: The trails are well-blazed and there are several short ones that run out to the roads around the park so get a map.

Dog Friendliness

Dogs are allowed in the picnic areas and on the hiking trails.

Traffic

Bikes are allowed and hunting is permitted.

Canine Swimming

Dogs must stay out of the lake but seek out the hidden pond near the boat ramp that is one of the best canine swimming holes anywhere.

Trail Time

Choose from an easy meander or head out for over an hour along the Fenton River or around the lake.

44
Denison Pequotsepos Nature Center

The Park

George Denison first sailed to America in 1631 at the age of 13 aboard the *Lion*, settling with his family in Roxbury, Massachusetts. He returned to England to fight with distinction under Oliver Cromwell before returning to New England and settling west of New London in 1654 in the heart of Pequot Indian Country. He became a staunch advocate for the Pequots and was granted 2,000 acres of tribal lands.

Upon his death in 1694, Denison split the lands among his descendants. In 1717 the old family home called Pequotsepos Manor burned on the eve of the wedding of George Denison III, the grandson who had inherited it and the adjoining 200 acres. He rebuilt west of the original site, salvaging some of the big charred oak beams from the frame of the older building. Today that home, now open to the public as a museum, is one of America's oldest homes continuously owned by the same family. The adjoining 300-acre nature preserve was established in 1946.

New London

Phone Number
- (860) 536-1216

Website
- www.dpnc.org

Admission Fee
- None for trails

Park Hours
- Dawn to dusk

Directions
- *Mystic*; Take Exit 90 from I-95 onto Route 27 North. Make a right on Jerry Browne Road and continue to a three-way stop. Turn right on Pequotsepos Road to Center on the left. Trail access can also be had on Maritime Drive off Coogan Boulevard opposite the Mystic Aquarium.

The Walks

Dogs are not generally allowed on the Nature Center trails but check in and see if they are not busy with wildlife programs that day and you might be permitted to sample these wooded trails, including the prime-time *Ledge Trail* and *Avalonia Trail* that feature dramatic rock outcroppings.

One place you can usually get on with your dog are the trails west of Pequotsepos Road, leaving from the trailhead opposite the Mystic Aquarium.

Your dog may not know what to make of "Plymouth Rock."

The *Stone Bridges Trail* moves steadily, but not oppressively, uphill to join the *Denison Farm Trail* loop where your dog can enjoy some open-air hiking on the edge of the historic farm fields. The trail passes an abandoned quarry and traverses stone walls in its one-way journey of about one mile.

Trail Sense: A trail guide is available from the Nature Center and the color-coded trails are well-marked.

Dog Friendliness
Dogs can use the trails with permission.
Traffic
Foot traffic only and your dog won't be welcome when it is crowded.
Canine Swimming
At the northern end of the *Stone Bridges Trail* the Pequotsepos Brook flows wide and soft for canine aquatics.
Trail Time
More than one hour.

45
Mansfield/
Nipmuck Trail

The Park

In 1676 Joshua, son of Uncas and Sachem of the Mohegans, bequeathed his hunting grounds in the heart of eastern Connecticut to sixteen men of Norwich. This historic tract comprised the present towns of Windham, Mansfield, Chaplin, Scotland, and part of Hampton. In this spirit of giving, Joshua's Tract Conservation and Historic Trust was organized and incorporated in 1966. Today the group has acquired 22 parcels of land in Mansfield.

The 37-mile *Nipmuck Trail* runs from Mansfield Hollow State Park north to the Nipmuck Forest. In the Town of Mansfield the footpath travels through three parks: Sawmill Preserve, Schoolhouse Brook Park and Fifty-Foot Cliff Preserve.

Tolland

Phone Number
- (860) 429-3015

Website
- www.mansfieldct.org/town/ departments/recreation/parks_ and_preserves/index.php

Admission Fee
- None

Park Hours
- Sunrise to sunset

Directions
- *Mansfield*; the best parking is at Schoolhouse Brook Park on Clover Mill Road west of Route 195 and behind the Mansfield Historical Society on the east side of Route 195.

The Walks

Situated in the middle of the trio and with the biggest parking lot (still limited to 8-10 vehicles), Schoolhouse Brook Park is your most convenient jumping off point for the Mansfield trails. In addition to the *Nipmuck Trail* linking the other parks, Schoolhouse Brook has an extensive trail system of its own with dozens of short, interlocking segments. Your dog will get the spectrum of hiking experiences here from short, brisk climbs to rocky passages to mucky pondside explorations.

At Sawmill Preserve your dog will find a sporty, heavily-wooded lollipop trail that leads over and around a forty-foot cliff topped by Wolf Rock. Follow the yellow-blazed trail off the *Nipmuck Trail* to complete your loop of just beyond one mile. Cliffs are also the dominant theme of Fifty-Foot Cliff Preserve; in this case a battleship-sized rock formation in dense woods. The hard-packed dirt trail moves along with little elevation change until you reach the short spur to the overlook. Stone walls and the adjacent University of Connecticut conifer collection are added bonuses of this leafy canine hike.

Although it looks like it would fall off the cliff with just a nudge, Wolf Rock will still be here long after your dog leaves.

Trail Sense: You can consult a detailed mapboard at Schoolhouse Brook; just follow the blue blazes and ignore the unmarked dirt bands that lead away from it in the other preserves.

Dog Friendliness
Dogs are allowed to enjoy these trails.

Traffic
Mountain bikes can navigate most of this terrain and the trails are popular with local dog walkers.

Canine Swimming
The ponds your dog finds on these hikes are more like marshes with troublesome access and plenty of vegetation. Bicentennial Pond on the north side of Clover Mill Road is suitable for a doggie dip if it's not swimming season.

Trail Time
About one hour in each of the parks.

46
Weir Farm
National Historic Site

The Park

In 1882, just as he was about to build a country retreat at Keene Valley in the Adirondacks, the 30-year-old Impressionist painter Julian Alden Weir was offered a 153-acre farm in Branchville in exchange for a painting he owned. Undaunted by the rocky landscape, Weir gladly took on the homestead called Land of Nod and began transforming the summer retreat into a creative refuge for friends and fellow artists over the next four decades.

In 1931 award-winning sculptor Mahonri Young, a grandson of Brigham Young, married Weir's daughter Dorothy. He lived and worked in a studio on the farm until his death in 1957.

Ridgefield artist Sperry Andrews had befriended Young and bought the property after the sculptor's death.

Fairfield

Phone Number
- (203) 834-1896

Website
- www.nps.gov/wefa/index.htm

Admission Fee
- None

Park Hours
- Grounds open dusk to dawn

Directions
- *Ridgefield*; from Route 7, about 10 miles north of Route 15 (the Merritt Parkway) and 10 miles south of I-84, take Route 102 West. Make the second left onto Old Branchville Road and left again onto Nod Hill Road and the Visitor Center is on top of the hill at 735 Nod Hill Road.

With his wife Doris, Sperry Andrews organized and spearheaded a grassroots preservation movement that ultimately led to saving much of Weir's original property. Today the 60-acre Weir Farm NHS is one of only two sites within the national park system that focus primarily on art and it is the only federal park unit in the State of Connecticut.

The Walks

No great destinations, no dramatic views - just a relaxing outing with your dog is what awaits the canine hiker at Weir Farm. Several short nature trails lead across open fields and into serene patches of forest. The main walk here is a grassy, paw-friendly exploration on the *Pond Trail* that leads to a farm pond and small waterfall through a typical 19th century Connecticut farmscape.

Your dog certainly won't collapse on the back seat from exhaustion after a day at Weir Farm but perhaps she'll return with a new found sense of serenity.

Trail Sense: The National Park Service provides a detailed map/brochure and blazes the trails.

Dog Friendliness

Dogs are allowed on the *Pond Trail* but not in the adjacent Weir Preserve of the Nature Conservancy.

Traffic

Walkers only at Weir Farm.

Canine Swimming

Your dog may be able to slip into the pond for a quick swim.

Trail Time

Less than one hour.

47
Wadsworth Falls
State Park

The Park

Clarence Seymour Wadsworth, heir to a 19th century China trade fortune and noted scholar and linguist in his own right, came to the rolling hills of western Middletown in 1900 to build a summer home. An early environmentalist Colonel Wadsworth (he had served in the New York National Guard), quickly became enamored of the falls on the Coginchaug River.

Historically the river had provided power for mills to manufacture textiles and gunpowder. Wadsworth spent his last 40 years working to preserve the beauty of the falls and when he died in 1941 his will established the Rockfall Corporation that gave 267 acres to the State to create the park.

Middlesex

Phone Number
- (860) 663-2030

Website
- www.ct.gov/dep/cwp/view.asp?a=2716&q=325274

Admission Fee
- None except seasonally on the weekends and holidays

Park Hours
- 8:00 a.m to sunset

Directions
- *Middletown*; on Route 157, south of Route 66 in the west end of town.

The Walks

The main trunk of the Wadsworth State Park trail system is a linear footpath of a little more than a mile that parallels the Coginchaug River. Wadsworth Falls is actually cut off from the rest of the park by a railroad line but you can reach the popular hydrospectacular by walking a short distance on Cherry Hill Road. You can also drive to the falls for a separate visit.

Even without Wadsworth Falls as a destination, the charms of the park trails can stand alone. The woods serve up massive hemlocks, cedars and stately oaks and a spectacular mountain laurel. The topography is varied and eye-catching, especially around Little Falls, a seasonal display on Wadsworth Brook. A variety of short chutes off the orange-blazed *Main Trail* enable you to take a different route on your return trip from the falls. This is all pretty easy going for your dog under the leafy canopy.

It doesn't get much better for your dog than an afternoon at Wadsworth Falls.

Trail Sense: The trails are blazed but there are many junctions so pay attention if you don't trust your dog to pick the way to go.

Dog Friendliness
Dogs are permitted on the trails and in the picnic areas.

Traffic
This is a busy park on a hot summer day but most folks come for the saucer-shaped swimming basin and not the trails. Bikes are allowed on most trails.

Canine Swimming
Your dog will enjoy a cool swim in the Coginchaug River when no fishermen are around. The waters in the plunge pool below Wadsworth Falls are too shallow for dog paddling but are refreshing nonetheless.

Trail Time
About one hour.

48
Rocky Neck
State Park

The Park

This area, bounded by a tidal river and an expansive salt marsh has long been known to settlers for its abundance of fish. A fish processing plant, in fact, operated here for many years. The operation is gone today, replaced by the fish hawks and shorebirds who feast on the rich waters.

Conservationists have long had Rocky Neck in their sights, with some of the land purchased privately as early as 1931 before the State of Connecticut acquired the park to create one of its most popular recreation destinations.

The Walks

Most of the beachgoers at Rocky Neck probably aren't even aware of the hiking available up on the bluff in

New London

Phone Number
- (860) 739-5471

Website
- www.ct.gov/dep/cwp/view.
asp?a=2716&q=325256

Admission Fee
- Yes during summer and on April, May and September weekends

Park Hours
- 8:00 a.m. to sunset

Directions
- *East Lyme*; take Exit 72 off I-95 to Route 156. Turn left to main park entrance or right to small trailhead lot on the left.

the woods on the other side of the parking lot. It is a quirky little trail system sandwiched between the Bride Brook and Fourmile River that packs a number of curiosities into a small area.

There are marsh views and an overlook 100 feet above Long Island Sound from the rock slab known as Tony's Nose. Your dog can poke around Baker's Cave, an opening in a jumble of rocks that was big enough to harbor Tory sympathizers during the American Revolution. In Shipyard Field your dog can take a break from woods walking and enjoy a succession meadow.

This is mild stuff for your dog on easy inclines as the park makes extensive use of old roads. You can pile together a bunch of trail segments to create a canine hiking loop of about two miles and in the off-season when the crowds disappear you can add the park roads and campground trails to your dog's day.

Trail Sense: A map is useful to decipher the tangle of short trails; also to help identify the rogue trails that pop up here and there.

Dog Friendliness
Dogs are permitted in the picnic areas and on the trails but not in the campground or on the beach.

Traffic
Almost everyone in the long line of cars in front of you is headed for the beach.

Canine Swimming
Not until the off-season when you can sneak down to the shore.

Trail Time
Less than one hour.

The open meadow in Shipyard Field is sure to be a highlight for your dog.

49
Topsmead
State Forest

The Park

Edith Morton Chase was an heir to the Chase Brass and Copper Company, one of the major players that made Waterbury the Brass Capital of the World. During the Civil War alone, Chase Brass and Copper manufactured fifty million cartridge cases.

In 1917, Edith Chase was given 16 acres atop Jefferson Hill by her father and she began to aggressively build up her financial inheritance and real estate holdings. In 1927 she named her summer retreat Topsmead Farm to reflect its location at the "top of the meadow."

The farm evolved and Edith Chase lived here with two companions, both sisters, until she died in 1972. Topsmead Farm was donated to the people of Connecticut, along with an endowment to maintain the estate "in a state of natural beauty."

Litchfield

Phone Number
- (860) 567-5694

Website
- ct.gov/dep/cwp/view.asp?A=2716&Q=325076

Admission Fee
- None

Park Hours
- 8:00 a.m. to sunset

Directions
- *Litchfield*; from Route 8 take Exit 42 and go west on Route 118 for two miles. Turn left onto Clark Road to the stop sign. Take a right at the stop sign then the first left onto Buell Road. The first right off Buell is the entrance to the park.

The Walks

Give your dog a break from those rocky, rugged trails found elsewhere in Connecticut and bring her to these grassy hills. Topsmead must look much the same as it did when Edith Chase last saw it 35 years ago. Your visit seems less like a day in the park than a calling on a relative in the English countryside.

A series of short hiking paths explore the landscaped grounds and your dog will be doing plenty of trotting on paw-friendly grass and down unpaved lanes. When you slip into the woods it is through an airy pinetum. An *Ecology Trail* interprets life in the Litchfield Hills.

There is plenty of room for your dog to stretch out at Topsmead State Forest.

Trail Sense: There are maps but no trail markings; wander the grounds like you own the place, not like a stranger who doesn't know her way around.

Dog Friendliness
Dogs are welcome to explore the estate, away from ground nesting birds.
Traffic
This is not a hectic place by any means; in fact there are no highway signs anywhere approaching Topsmead Forest so you don't just stumble your way into the park.
Canine Swimming
A secluded pond is an ideal spot for a languid doggie swim.
Trail Time
Less than one hour.

50
Dennis Hill
State Park

The Park

The Dennis of Dennis Hill was Frederick Shepard Dennis, one of the first physicians to observe the effect of penicillin mold on bacteria in culture and a pioneer in introducing Joseph Lister's antiseptic methods to the United States. The New York surgeon married a local girl and built a 240-acre estate on this windswept, 1627-foot extinct volcano.

Dennis entertained the rich and powerful of the day here, Presidents Theodore Roosevelt and William Taft among them. He kept a $25,000 check on display, given to him by Andrew Carnegie to perform a particularly tricky operation.

Litchfield

Phone Number
- (860) 482-1817

Website
- www.ct.gov/dep/cwp/view.asp?A=2716&Q=325186

Admission Fee
- None

Park Hours
- 8:00 a.m. to sunset

Directions
- *Norfolk*; from the center of town on Route 44, go south on Route 272 to the park on the left.

After Dr. Dennis' death in 1934 the estate was donated to the State of Connecticut. The barren hill was used for planespotting during World War II and remains undeveloped today.

The Walks

If you are looking for a place to get away from the madding crowds with your dog, this could be it. There are no recreational facilities, bikes are not allowed and the picnic area only has three tables. If the pavilion isn't rented out you may be the only one in the park more often than not.

Canine hiking takes place on the *Gazebo Loop* that covers almost two miles on an old carriage road. It is uphill enough that your dog will look forward to reaching the overlooks at the stone-and-wood gazebo. Whereas Dennis Hill is open, this hike takes place completely under a leafy canopy. Frederick Dennis laid out the trails himself, reforesting the hills with 5,000 pines and trees from all over the world. His fern collection was considered the most complete in New England so keep an eye out in the understory.

Trail Sense: Stick to the woods road and it will take you around.

Dog Friendliness
Dogs are allowed across Dennis Hill.

Traffic
Little if any.

Canine Swimming
None.

Trail Time
About one hour.

Bring your dog to Dennis Hill for the views; stay for the hiking. The Dennis home was gutted by fire but the stone exterior remains. An exterior stairway once led to a viewing platform on the roof.

51
Goodwin
State Forest

The Park

The forest, that includes more than 2,000 acres, is named for James L. Goodwin, a forester who operated a tree farm on the property from 1921 to 1964. The forest borders Pine Acres Pond that was created in 1933 when a dam was built on Cedar Swamp Brook in order to flood the existing swamp.

The Goodwin Conservation Center overlooks the pond, serving as an interpretive museum explaining natural sciences and forestry.

The Walks

The blue-blazed *Natchaug Trail* begins its 18.7-mile journy here. It is a narrow, pick-your-way sort of trail for dogs around roots and small stones as you move up the eastern shore of Pine Acres Pond. Your dog won't have to trot the entire 18 miles but there are no easy strolls in the Goodwin State Forest.

Another long-distance trail your dog can hike here is the *Air Line Trail*, built on the old railbed of the New York and New England Railroad that operated from 1873 to

Windham

Phone Number
- (860) 455-9534

Website
- www.ct.gov/dep/cwp/view.asp?a=2716&q=325188

Admission Fee
- None

Park Hours
- Dusk to dawn

Directions
- *Hampton*; the entrance is on Potter Road, off Route 6 between Routes 198 and 97.

Only small dogs will be able to dog-paddle in Pine Acres Pond when the pond lillies are in bloom.

1955. The service was nicknamed the "Air Line" since it was laid out in the most direct route from Boston to New York. Envisioned as a footpath from the Rhode Island border to the Connecticut River the stretch through Goodwin forest is part of the South Section that connects East Hampton to Willimantic. Your dog can expect crushed stone, gravel, and ballast under foot, wooded the entire way.

Trail Sense: The trails are well-blazed and a map can sometimes be had at the trailhead or in the Conservation Center.

Dog Friendliness
Dogs are allowed on trails across the Goodwin State Forest.
Traffic
These are not heavily-used trails but bikes and horses and skiers can use the *Air Line Trail*.
Canine Swimming
The maximum depth for Pine Acres Lake is only seven feet and a Great Dane can walk across most of its 130 acres. Subsequently it is heavily vegetated with bladderwort, pondweed and pond lillies. Even around the boat launch there is little open water for your dog to stretch his swimming legs.
Trail Time
At least one hour.

52

Putnam Memorial State Park

The Park

Major General Israel Putnam grew larger than life during a career fighting in the frontier and in the French and Indian War. He is said to have survived a burning at the stake, an imprisonment in Montreal and a shipwreck off the coast of Cuba.

During the Revolution, however, after distinguished service at Bunker Hill, he lost Forts Clinton and Montgomery in the Hudson Highlands and by the winter of 1778, in his sixtieth year, he was given the less rigorous task of commanding the camp at Redding. Here "Old Put's" most notable achievement was squelching a looming mutiny as soldiers threatened to march on Hartford for more supplies and food.

A stone obelisk was erected by the state in 1888 to honor the men who suffered through an exceptionally severe winter here. The dramatic equestrian statue of General Putnam at the park's entrance is the work of nearby resident Anna Hyatt Huntington.

Fairfield

Phone Number
- (203) 938-2285

Website
- ct.gov/dep/cwp/view.asp?a=2716&q=325250&depNav_GID=1650

Admission Fee
- None

Park Hours
- 8:00 a.m. to sunset

Directions
- *Redding*; on Route 58 at the intersection with Route 107, three miles south of Route 302 and nine miles north of Route 136.

In this attractive hillside setting, a stone memorial remembers the hardships of Continental Arny soldiers during the winter of 1778.

The Walks

A shady, one-mile *Interpretive Trail* describes the camp layout and leads past the reconstructed quarters and stone firebacks of "Connecticut's Valley Forge." The crumbling chimneys and other traces of buildings are the most discernable of any remaining American Revolutionary camp. This is an easy trip for your dog on wide, unpaved roads as it doubles back past foundation ruins, a rock shelter and memorials.

Across the road in the day-use area your dog can enjoy relaxed trotting across several miles of unmarked dirt paths and closed roads through wooded hillsides.

Trail Sense: A park map will guide you to the historical highlights but nothing is marked on the ground.

Dog Friendliness

Dogs are allowed on the trails and in the picnic areas.

Traffic

Unless it is a special event, visitors come to these historic grounds at a trickle but the trail/roads in the park are open to motorized vehicles.

Canine Swimming

Your dog may be able to find open water in the normally vegetated Putnam Park Pond but the real find for water-loving dogs is a small woodland pond with grassy banks across from the stone monument.

Trail Time

About one hour.

119

53
Mount Tom
State Park

The Park

The local Bantam Indians long used Mount Tom as hunting grounds. In the 1920s it became one of the first parks in the state park system. The summit of Mount Tom is 1325 feet above sea level, 125 feet higher than its Massachusetts counterpart.

The Walks

The trail to the top of Mount Tom is less than one mile long but your dog will get a workout here, gaining about 500 feet in elevation in a half-mile. There is no warm-up and, with the exception of a single switchback, straight up. Your dog will start on a cobble road that turns just rocky before succumbing to paw-friendly dirt.

Litchfield

Phone Number
- (860) 567-8870

Website
- www.ct.gov/dep/cwp/view.
asp?A=2716&Q=325244

Admission Fee
- None except seasonally on the weekends and holidays

Park Hours
- 8:00 a.m. to sunset

Directions
- *Litchfield*; on Route 202 west of Bantam. Take Route 4, Exit 39, off I-84 to Route 118 into Litchfield and Route 202.

Once on top you don't have any views without climbing the tower. Three people and three dogs would make the tower observation deck very crowded so if you are coming to Mount Tom for the views - and they are some of the best in the state - don't come on a crisp fall weekend.

You can take an alternate trail down, a more traditional pick-your-way footpath and use the park road to close your loop.

Trail Sense: The trails are blazed in yellow but you can certainly find your way to the tower. Once on top, ignore the unmarked dirt trails that run off into the woods - these lead to potentially dangerous drop-offs for your dog.

Your dog will need to climb higher than this first floor window to see
anything from the Mount Tom tower.

Dog Friendliness

Dogs are not allowed on the beach but can hike the trails and hang in the
picnic area.

Traffic

Foot traffic only; Mount Tom can be popular during hawk migration.

Canine Swimming

Mount Tom Pond is a super doggie swimming hole when the beach is closed;
its pond-fed waters are cool and clear. Otherwise your dog can get to the
water around the edges of the park but stay off the private property.

Trail Time

About one hour.

54
Haystack Mountain State Park

The Park

Known for its cool breezes, Norfolk long-ago picked up the reputation as the "Icebox of Connecticut" and began attracting wealthy vacationers arriving on the New York-to-Pittsfield rail line. In June the area was renowned for its luxuriant displays of mountain laurel.

The dominant topographical feature for the holiday crowd was Haystack Mountain on the north edge of town. It's distinctive shape is readily recognizable today and in the 1800s, with its hillside shorn of timber used for charcoal, it really resembled a haystack.

Robbins Battell built a carriage road to the 1,716-foot summit and his daughter, Ellen Battell Stoeckel donated the land for a state park in 1929.

The Walks

If the entrance road is open, the paved portion takes you to within a half-mile of the summit. Your dog hike at this point begins on a lovely flat path into the woods. When the climbing begins in earnest,

---

Litchfield

Phone Number
- (860) 482-1817

Website
- www.ct.gov/dep/cwp/view.asp?A=2716&Q=325216

Admission Fee
- None

Park Hours
- 8:00 a.m. to sunset

Directions
- *Norfolk*; on the west side of Route 272, just north of the intersection with Route 44 in the center of town.

This pond may, or may not, be your starting point for the hike up Haystack Mountain but your dog will certainly want to finish her day here.

wide stone steps built into the slope ease the trip up Haystack Mountain. Even novice canine hikers will be able to tag the summit without testing the limits of exhaustion.

If the entrance road is closed, simply extend your trail time by heading up the switchbacking lane. Even if the road is open, non-weekend traffic is light so parking at the turnout by the pond and heading up the macadam creates a fine outing with your dog.

Not every dog will want to climb the open grate steps to the top of the tower on the Haystack Mountain summit.

Trail Sense: No maps and even with a mystery mix of blue and yellow blazes there is little chance of getting lost on the way to the tower.

Dog Friendliness
Dogs are allowed to hike on Haystack Mountain.
Traffic
If the leaves aren't pretty colors this is not a heavily used park.
Canine Swimming
Pull over by the pond along the entrance road for a refreshing swim for your dog.
Trail Time
Less than one hour.

55
Hopeville Pond State Park

The Park

The Mohegan Indians saw the Pachaug River as a great resource for fish, teeming with eels and shad. The first British settlers saw the tumbling waters as a source of power for grist mills and sawmills. In 1711 Stephen Gates was presented with 14 acres here in return for his services as a surveyor and he built the first mills that were to change the character of the river.

A century later wool was being manufactured on the Pachaug and John Slater built a satinet mill faced with   local granite to produce imitation satin. He named his new enterprise Hope Mill and its success spawned a thriving village that came to be known as Hopeville.

New London

Phone Number
- (860) 376-0313

Website
- www.ct.gov/dep/cwp/view.
asp?a=2716&q=325218

Admission Fee
- None except seasonally on the weekends and holidays

Park Hours
- 8:00 a.m. to sunset

Directions
- *Griswold*; from I-95, take Exit 86. Follow Hopeville Road to Route 201 to the park entrance on the right.

The mill was destroyed by fire in 1881 and never rebuilt. Two decades later flames roared through the remaining settlement leaving it in ruins. A few years later, in 1908, the gristmill that had operated since 1711 also burned and the area began to revert to forestland. The site became part of the Federal Government's large purchase of land in Eastern Connecticut during the Depression of the 1930s.

The Walks

There are no great destinations in store at Hopeville Pond but it is a good place to get out in the woods with your dog. The *Nehantic Trail* runs from the park off to the Pachaug State Forest. You will need to retrace your pawprints on this exploration.

The best time to visit Hopeville Pond is in the quiet off-season when the camp is closed and your dog can explore the *Nature Trail* and enjoy the easy access to the water from the beach. Most of this route travels on paw-friendly pine straw through a pine plantation developed by the Civilian Conservation Corps in the 1930s.

Trail Sense: A mapboard at the parking lot provides orientation for the park. You could follow the *Nehantic Trail* that leaves across Route 201 just with the blazes if you had to.

Dog Friendliness

Dogs are not allowed on the swimming beach or in the campground from April 30 to September 30.

Traffic

Most of the park users come for the ballfields, camping or swimming in the pond so you could slip away onto the *Nehantic Trail* unnoticed.

Canine Swimming

The open waters of Hopeville Pond are easily accessed for your dog.

Trail Time

Less than an hour, although you can make a day of it with your dog on the *Nehantic Trail* if so desired.

If there are no dogs in Heaven,
then when I die I want to go where they went.
-Anonymous

56
Penwood State Park

The Park

In 1895, Curtis Veeder, an electrical engineer, invented a Cyclometer to record the miles traveled on a bicycle. He sold it to the bicycle-crazed America with the slogan, *It's Nice to Know How Far You Go*. The Cyclometer's success led to a full line of Veeder counting devices, including the modern tachometer, odometer and gas station pump.

Curtis and Louise Veeder came to their hilltop in the Talcott Mountains to enjoy nature (their West End home in Hartford is now the headquarters of the Connecticut Historical Society). He named their retreat 'Penwood' partly because his ancestors came from Pennsylvania and partly because the name Veeder is Dutch for 'pen.'

Ardent hikers, the couple laid out most of the hilltop trails themselves. At night, Veeder would make exacting measurements of the sky, creating detailed maps and establishing a true meridian line from the exact psoition of a star. After his death in 1943, the property was willed to the state for the enjoyment of all its people.

Hartford

Phone Number
- (860) 242-1158

Website
- www.ct.gov/dep/cwp/view.asp?A=2716&Q=325248

Admission Fee
- None

Park Hours
- 8:00 a.m. to sunset

Directions
- *Bloomfield*; from Route 202 follow Route 10 North to Route 185. Make a right and the park entrance is on the left at the top of the hill.

The Walks

Aside from an old picnic pavilion, Penwood State Park has no amenities. Park roads are closed or beat up - or both. The boardwalk has rotted away. Nothing to attract visitors. In short, a great rough-and-tumble place to hike with your dog.

Some dog owners simply use the macadam roads for trails. These roads are deeply shaded by thick forests and can be followed to the overgrown banks of Lake Louise on top of the ridge. The main hiking trail in the park is the blue-blazed *Metacomet Trail* that slices across the entirety of Penwood. Although long, it is fairly easy going for just about any dog.

Below the ridge at the inside parking area you will find large grass fields ringed by pine trees that make a great spot for a game of fetch.

Trail Sense: There are small wooden hiking signs pointing down various paths but without studying a map it will be a mystery what they lead to. An information board in the parking lot outside the gate may be of help.

Dog Friendliness
Dogs are allowed throughout Penwood State Park.
Traffic
Mostly mountain bikers on the *Metacomet Trail*;
Canine Swimming
Access to Lake Louise and Shadow Pond is virtually nil and inviting Gale Pond is private.
Trail Time
More than one hour.

57
Lantern Hill

The Park

On a clear day your dog can see five states -- New York, Connecticut, Massachusetts, Rhode Island, and Vermont - from the top of Lantern Hill. Sassacus, whose legendary warring raids on rival tribes and British colonists led to the Pequot War in 1636, was said to have used the summit to scout the waters and approaching roads.

But the name of the 490-foot hill derives more from the ability to see it than its views. The bare granite peak is flecked with chunks of quartz that glisten in the sun so Lantern Hill could be used by mariners approaching the coast.

New London

Phone Number
- None

Website
- None

Admission Fee
- None

Park Hours
- Sunrise to sunset

Directions
- *North Stonington*; Roadside parking is available at the trailhead on Wintechog Hill Road just south of Route 2, just east of Route 214 and the Foxwoods Casino.

The hill is alternately known as Tar Barrel Hill dating to the War of 1812. British warships were wreaking havoc along the Connecticut coast, having sacked Essex. To protect its town Stonington residents hauled massive hogsheads of tar to the top of Lantern Hill (think about their efforts as you hike to the top with your dog) so they could fuel signal fires. On August 11, 1814 the tar barrel lanterns were ignited as the British fleet appeared in the harbor. Properly alerted, the townspeople retreated and the militia massed in defense. British cannon balls fell to little purpose and the assault was abandoned.

The Walks

You will get right down to it on Lantern Hill. The climb from the trailhead on Wintechog Hill is steady but not killer. It will get your dog's attention, however, as will the well-worn, packed-dirt and stone path. The serpentine trail soon emerges on the side of the hill where your dog will be eyeball to eyeball with the Foxwoods Casino and the Mashantucket Pequot Museum with its 185-foot viewing spire.

After tagging the summit of Lantern Hill you can return to your vehicle for a round trip of less than 1.5 miles or continue on the blue-blazed *Narragansett Trail* down the other side of the hill and onto Wintechog Hill. For additional trail time you can take the dog down the blazed *Pequot Trail* that joins Lantern Hill shortly after you begin and runs through the casino complex.

Trail Sense: The trails are blazed but no maps are available. There are plenty of unmarked trails around Lantern Hill so pay attention to the blazes if you are not of a mind to explore.

Dog Friendliness
Dogs are allowed to climb on Lantern Hill.

Traffic
The limited parking keeps traffic light; beware of hunters in fall.

Canine Swimming
None on Lantern Hill but you can reach ponds with bigger journeys on the long-distance trails.

Trail Time
Less than one hour to tag the summit and return.

Camping With Your Dog In Connecticut

Note: Dogs are not permitted in any Connecticut state park campground.

Litchfield County

Branch Brook Campground
Thomaston
At 435 Watertown Road, west of Route 8, Exit 38. On Route 6, south of CT 109.
open April 1 to November 1   (860) 283-8144

Gentile's Campground
Plymouth
At 262 Mount Tobe Road, east of Route 8, Exit 36. Turn right at Huntingdon Avenue, left at Thomaston Avenue and right on CT 262.
http://www.gentilescampground.com/
open April 1 to November 1   (860) 283-8437

Hemlock Hill Camp Resort
Litchfield
At 118 Hemlock Hill Road off Milton Road, 4 miles from US 202. Take Exit 42 from Route 8 and follow CT 118 West to Litchfield Center and 202 West.
http://www.hemlockhillcamp.com/
open late April to late October (860) 567-2267

Lone Oak Campsites
East Canaan
On Route 44, 4 miles east of town.
http://www.loneoakcampsites.com/
open mid-April to mid-October   (860) 824-7051

Mohawk Campground
Goshen
On Route 4 east of Route 43 and west of Route 63.
open early May to early October   (860) 283-1012

Valley In The Pines
Goshen
At 36 Lucas Road off Milton Road, south of Route 4 west of town.
open mid-April to late October   (860) 491-2032

White Memorial Family Campground
Litchfield
At 123 North Shore Road off Bissell Road from Route 202, two miles west of Route 63.
www.whitememorialcc.org/
open May 1 to mid-October   (860) 567-0089

White Pines Campsites
Barkhamsted
At 232 Old North Road off Wallens Hill Road from Wallens Street in Winsted Center, east of Route 8.
http://www.whitepinescamp.com/
open April 1 to October 31   (860) 379-0124

Middlesex County

Little City Campground
Higganum
On Little City Road south of Candlewood Hill Road, west of town.
May 1 to October 1   (860) 345-4886

Markham Meadows Campground
East Hampton
From town go south on Main Street to Route 16 East, Middletown Avenue. Turn right on Tartia Road and left on Markham Road to campground.
http://www.markhammeadows.com/
open mid-May 1 to mid-October   (315) 267-9738

Nelson's Family Campground
East Hampton
Go north from town on Main Street to Lake Road and left on Mott Hill Road to campground on left.
http://www.nelsonscampground.com/
open mid-April to mid-October   (866) 445-6520

Riverdale Farm Campsite
Clinton
From Exit 62 off I-95, take a right onto Duck Hole Road. Take the first left onto a small bridge and then a left off of the bridge for two miles to 111 River Road.
http://www.riverdalefarmcampsite.com/
open late April to Columbus Day   (860) 669-5388

Wolf's Den Family Campground
East Haddam
On Route 82, four miles east of town.
http://www.wolfsdencampground.com/
open early May to late October   (860) 873-9681

New Haven County

Totoket Valley RV Park
North Branford
On Route 80, Foxon Road, 3.5 miles from I-91, Exit 8.
http://www.totoketrvpark.com/
open year-round   (203) 484-0099

New London County

Aces High RV Park
East Lyme
On Route 161, three miles north of I-95, Exit 74.
http://aceshighrvpark.com/
open year-round   (860) 739-8858

Acorn Acres Campground
Bozrah
Southwest of town at 135 Lake Road, south of Route 2.
http://www.acornacrescampsites.com/
open early May to Columbus Day   (860) 859-1020

Camp Niantic-By-The-Atlantic
Niantic
At 271 Main Street (Route 156).
open mid-April to mid-October   (860) 739-9308

Campers World
Jewett City
Exit I-395 onto route 201 and go to first stop sign and turn right on Edmond Road. Turn left on Nowakowski Road to the campground.
http://www.campersworldcampground.com/hq.pl
open April 15 to October 15   (860) 376-2340

Circle "C" Campground
Voluntown
On Bailey Pond Road, right at the end of Gallup Homestead Road. Take Exit 85 off I-395 to oute 138 East to Route 49 North to Brown Road and right onto Gallup Homestead Road.
open late April to early October   (860) 564-4534

Countryside RV Park
Griswold
East of town via Voluntown Road (Route 138) and right on Route 201 to left on Cook Hill Road to campground.
http://www.countrysidecampground.com/home/
open May 1 to Columbus Day   (860) 376-0029

Deer Haven Campground
Lisbon
Exit onto Route 169 North from I-395; after 1/2 mile, turn left onto Kendell Road Extension and bear left onto Strnad Road. Take a left at the top of the hill to the campground.
http://www.deerhavencampground.net/
open April 15 to Columbus Day   (860) 376-1081

Hidden Acres Family Campground
Preston
Take Exit 85 off I-395 and go south 1 mile on Route 164. Turn right on George Palmer Road and continue 3 miles to campground, bearing right all the way.
http://www.hiddenacrescamp.com/
open mid-May to mid-October   (860) 887-9633

Highland Orchards Resort Park
North Stonington
Take Exit 85 off I-395 and go south 1 mile on Route 164. Turn right on George Palmer Road and continue 3 miles to campground, bearing right all the way.
http://www.highlandorchards.com/
open March 15 to December 15   (860) 599-5101

Indianfield Campground
Salem
West of I-395, take Route 82 to Route 354 North, Old Colchester Road to campground at 306.
open mid-April to end of October   (860) 859-1320

Lake Williams Campground
Lebanon
Take Route 85 north of Colchester for 3.5 miles and turn right (east) onto Route 207. Travel 2.4 miles to campground on left.
open mid-April to early October   (860) 642-7761

Laurel Lock Family Campground
Oakdale
West of I-395; take Route 163 to Lake Road and go west making a left on Cottage Road to campground.
open May 1 to Columbus Day   (860) 859-1424

M.H.G. RV Park
North Stonington
On Route 184, north of I-95.
open year-round   (860) 535-0501

Mystic KOA
North Stonington
From Exit 92 off I-95 take Route 49, Pendleton Hill Road, north.
open year-round   (860) 599-8944

Nature's Campsites
Voluntown
On Route 49, seven miles north of Route 138, east of I-395.
http://www.naturescampsites.com/
open May 1 to October 15   (860) 376-4203

Odetah Campground
Bozrah
Take I-395 North to Exit 81W. Go 2 miles west on Route 2 to Exit 23. Turn left at bottom of ramp. Go straight at intersection to campground on right.
http://www.odetah.com/home/
open May 1 to October 31   (860) 889-4144

Pequot Ledge Campground
Oakdale
Take Exit 80 West off I-395 onto Route 82. Drive about 5 miles to right onto Church Road to end. Turn left to campground on right.
http://www.pequotledge.com/
open April 15 to October 15   (860) 859-0682

Ross Hill Park Family Campground
Lisbon
Take Route 138, Newent Road, east of town and turn left and go north on Ross Hill Road to campground.
http://www.rosshillpark.com/
open year-round   (860) 376-9606

Salem Farms Campground
Salem
At 39 Alexander Road off Salem Road west of Route 11, Exit 5.
http://www.salemfarmscampground.com/
open May 1 to Columbus Day   (860) 859-2320

Salt Rock Campground
Baltic
At 173 Scotland Road (Route 97), two miles north of I-395, Exit 83.
open mid-April to mid-October   (860) 822-0884

Seaport Campground
Old Mystic
On Route 184, north of I-95, Exit 89.
http://www.seaportcampground.com/
open mid-April to October 15   (860) 536-4044

Strawberry Park Resort Campground
Preston
At 42 Pierce Road off Route 165 from Route 164 and Route 2.
http://www.strawberrypark.net/
open year-round   (860) 886-1944

Water's Edge Family Campground
Lebanon
On Leonard Bridge Road off Route 207, three miles from Route 85.
http://www.watersedgecampground.com/
open mid-April to mid-October   (860) 642-7470

Witch Meadow Lake Campground
Salem
At 139 Witch Meadow Road off Exit 5 from Route 11.
http://www.witchmeadowcampground.com/
open May 1 to early October   (860) 859-1542

Tolland County

Del-Aire Campground
Tolland
At 704 Shenipsit Lake Road off Route 30 from I-84.
open May 1 to October 15   (860) 875-8325

Mineral Springs Family Campground
Stafford Springs
On Leonard Road one mile north of Route 319, east of Route 32 north of I-84, Exit 70.
http://www.mineralspringscampground.com/
open May 1 to October 15   (860) 684-2993

Moosemeadow Camping Resort
West Willington
On Moosemeadow Road off Route 74, four miles east of I-84, Exit 69.
http://www.moosemeadow.com/
open mid-April to mid-October   (860) 429-7451

Roaring Brook Campground
Stafford Springs
Off Route 190 from I-84, Exit 72.
http://www.roaringbrookcampground.com/
open April to October 15   (860) 684-7086

Windham County

Beaver Pines Campground
Woodstock
From Exit 73 of I-84 take Route 190 East to Route 171 to Route 197 and north on Route 198 1.5 miles.
http://www.beaverpinescampground.com/
open mid-April to mid-October   (860) 974-0110

Brialee RV & Tent Park
Ashford
At 174 Laurel Lane, off Perry Hill; off Route 89 north of Route 44.
http://www.brialee.net/
open April 1 to October 31   (860) 429-8359

Chamberlain Lake Campground
Woodstock
From Exit 73 of I-84 take Route 190 East to Route 171 to Route 197.
open May 1 to Columbus Day   (860) 974-0567

Charlie Brown Campground
Eastford
At 98 Chaplin Road (Route 198), seven miles north of Route 6.
http://www.ctcampground.com/
open mid-April to mid-October   (860) 974-0142

Hide-Away-Cove Family Campground
East Killingly
At 1060 North Road, north of town and Route 101, east of I-395..
http://www.hideawaycovecampground.com/
open May 1 to early October   (860) 774-1128

Highland Campground
Scotland
On Toleration Road east of Route 97, south of Route 14, west of I-395.
http://www.highlandcampground.com/
open late April to late October   (860) 423-5684

Nickerson Park
Chaplin
At 1036 Phoenixville Pike (Route 198), four miles north of Route 6.
http://www.nickersonpark.com/
open year-round   (860) 455-0007

Peppertree Camping
Eastford
At 146 Chaplin Road (Route 198), north of Route 6.
http://www.peppertreecamping.com/
open mid-April to mid-October   (860) 455-0007

River Bend Campground
Oneco
At 41 Pond Street off Route 14A, 5.5 miles east of I-395, Exit 88.
http://www.riverbendcamp.com/
open late May to Columbus Day   (860) 564-3440

Stateline Campresort
East Killingly
On Route 101, 5 miles east of I-395, Exit 93.
http://www.statelinecampresort.com/
open year-round   (860) 774-3016

Sterling Park Campground
Sterling
On Gibson Hill Road, six miles east of I-395 via Route 14A.
http://www.sterlingcampground.com/
open mid-April to mid-October   (860) 564-8777

West Thompson Lake Campground
North Grosvenordale
On Reardon Road, north of Route 193 west of I-395, Exit 98..
open late May to mid-September   (860) 923-3121

Your Dog At The Beach

It is hard to imagine many places a dog is happier than at a beach. Whether romping on the sand, digging a hole, jumping in the water or just lying in the sun, every dog deserves a day at the beach. But all too often dog owners stopping at a sandy stretch of beach are met with signs designed to make hearts - human and canine alike - droop: NO DOGS ON BEACH.

Below is a summary of rules for dogs at some of Connecticut's many beaches...

Clinton
203-669-6901

Town Beach
NO DOGS ALLOWED ON BEACH

East Haven
203-468-3367

Town Beach
DOGS ALLOWED ON BEACH FROM LABOR DAY TO MEMORIAL DAY

East Lyme
860-739-5471

Rocky Neck State Park
DOGS NOT ALLOWED ON BEACH

Fairfield
203-256-3000

Jennings Beach
DOGS ON BEACH FROM OCT 1 - APRIL 1
Penfield Beach
DOGS ON BEACH FROM OCT 1 - APRIL 1
Richards Beach
DOGS ON BEACH FROM OCT 1 - APRIL 1
Sasco Beach
DOGS ON BEACH FROM OCT 1 - APRIL 1
Southport Beach
DOGS ON BEACH FROM OCT 1 - APRIL 1

Groton
860-536-5680

Bluff Point Park
DOGS ALLOWED ON BEACH SEPT 16 - APR 14
Esker Point Beach
DOGS ALLOWED ON BEACH EXCEPT DURING NIGHTS WITH CONCERTS
Main Street Beach
DOGS ALLOWED ON BEACH

Madison
203-245-5623
203-245-1817

203-245-5623

203-245-5623

East Wharf Beach
NO DOGS ALLOWED ON BEACH
Hammonasset Beach State Park
NO DOGS ALLOWED ON BEACH
Surf Club Beach
NO DOGS ALLOWED ON BEACH
West Wharf Beach
NO DOGS ALLOWED ON BEACH

Milford	Gulf Beach
203-783-3201	*NO DOGS ALLOWED ON BEACH*
203-735-4311	Silver Sands State Beach
	NO DOGS ALLOWED ON BEACH
203-783-3201	Walnut Beach
	NO DOGS ALLOWED ON BEACH
New Haven	Lighthouse Point Park
203-946-8790	*NO DOGS ALLOWED ON BEACH*
New London	Ocean Beach Park
800-510-7263	*NO DOGS ALLOWED ON BEACH*
Old Lyme	Sound View Beach
860-434-1605 x235	*NO DOGS ALLOWED ON BEACH*
Old Saybrook	Harvey's Beach
860-395-3123	*NO DOGS ALLOWED ON BEACH*
	Town Beach
	NO DOGS ALLOWED ON BEACH
Stamford	Cove Island Park
203-977-4054	*NON-RESIDENTS ARE DISCOURAGED FROM USING THE BEACH*
	Cummings Park
	NON-RESIDENTS ARE DISCOURAGED FROM USING THE BEACH
Stonington	Dubois Beach
860-535-5060	*NO DOGS ALLOWED ON BEACH*
Stratford	Long Beach
203-385-4020	*NO DOGS ALLOWED ON BEACH*
	Russian Beach
	NO DOGS ALLOWED ON BEACH
	Short Beach Park
	NO DOGS ALLOWED ON BEACH
West Haven	Altschuler Beach
203-937-3651	*NO DOGS ALLOWED ON BEACH*
	Bradley Point Park
	NO DOGS ALLOWED ON BEACH
	Dawson Beach
	NO DOGS ALLOWED ON BEACH
	Morse Beach
	NO DOGS ALLOWED ON BEACH
	Oak Street Beach
	NO DOGS ALLOWED ON BEACH
	Peck Beach
	NO DOGS ALLOWED ON BEACH
	Seabluff Beach
	NO DOGS ALLOWED ON BEACH

Westport	Burying Hill Beach
203-341-1038	**DOGS ALLOWED ON BEACH NOV 1 TO APR 30**
	Canal Beach
	DOGS ALLOWED ON BEACH NOV 1 TO APR 30
	Compo Beach
	DOGS ALLOWED ON BEACH NOV 1 TO APR 30
	Old Mill Beach
	DOGS ALLOWED ON BEACH NOV 1 TO APR 30
	Sherwood Island State Park
	LEASHED DOGS ALLOWED IN PARK OCT 1 TO APRIL 14

Tips For Taking Your Dog To The Beach

- The majority of dogs can swim and love it, but dogs entering the water for the first time should be tested; never throw a dog into the water. Start in shallow water and call your dog's name - or try to coax him in with a treat or toy. Always keep your dog within reach.

- Another way to introduce your dog to the water is with a dog that already swims and is friendly with your dog. Let your dog follow his friend.

- If your dog begins to doggie paddle with his front legs only, lift his hind legs and help him float. He should quickly catch on and will keep his back end up.

- Swimming is a great form of exercise, but don't let your dog overdo it. He will be using new muscles and may tire quickly.

- Be careful of strong tides that are hazardous for even the best swimmers.

- Cool ocean water is tempting to your dog. Do not allow him to drink too much sea water. Salt in the water will make him sick. Salt and other minerals found in the ocean can damage your dog's coat so regular bathing is essential.

- Check with a lifeguard for daily water conditions - dogs are easy targets for jellyfish and sea lice.

- Dogs can get sunburned, especially short-haired dogs and ones with pink skin and white hair. Limit your dog's exposure when the sun is strong and apply sunblock to his ears and nose 30 minutes before going outside.

- If your dog is out of shape, don't encourage him to run on the sand, which is strenuous exercise and a dog that is out of shape can easily pull a tendon or ligament.

Index To Parks, Trails & Open Space

How To Pet A Dog
Tickling tummies slowly and gently works wonders.
Never use a rubbing motion; this makes dogs bad-tempered.
A gentle tickle with the tips of the fingers is all that is necessary
to induce calm in a dog. I hate strangers who go up to dogs with their
hands held to the dog's nose, usually palm towards themselves.
How does the dog know that the hand doesn't hold something horrid?
The palm should always be shown to the dog and go straight
down to between the dog's front legs and tickle gently with
a soothing voice to accompany the action.
Very often the dog raises its back leg in a scratching movement,
it gets so much pleasure from this.
-Barbara Woodhouse

Made in the USA
Middletown, DE
20 February 2020